Himalaya and Karakoram

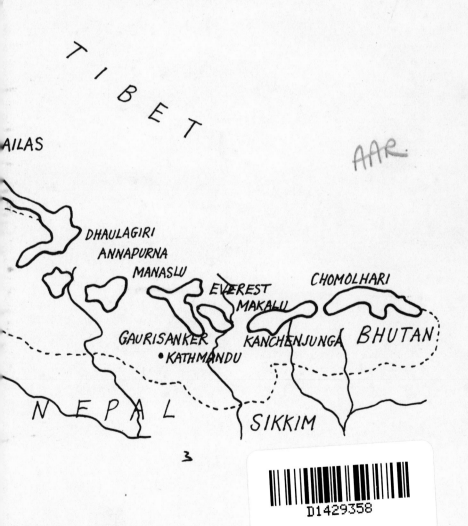

T I B E T

AILAS

AAR.

DHAULAGIRI
ANNAPURNA
MANASLU
EVEREST
MAKALU
CHOMOLHARI
GAURISANKER
KANCHENJUNGA
BHUTAN
• KATHMANDU

N E P A L

SIKKIM

3

HIGH AMBITION

A Biography of Reinhold Messner

by

RONALD FAUX

LONDON
VICTOR GOLLANCZ LTD
1982

British Library Cataloguing in Publication Data
Faux, Ronald
   High ambition.
   1. Messner, Reinhold   2. Mountaineers—
   Italy—Biography
   I. Title
   796.5'22'0924   GV199.92.M/

ISBN 0-575-03069-0

Printed in Great Britain by
St Edmundsbury Press
Bury St Edmunds, Suffolk

For Frances

ACKNOWLEDGEMENTS

This biography was written after I reported the ascent of Everest by Reinhold Messner and Peter Habeler in spring of 1978 for *The Times*. It is based on extensive interviews with Messner and study of his diaries and records. I am greatly indebted to Audrey Salkeld, the mountaineering historian and translator of a number of Messner's books, to Trevor Mann, climber and specialist in German, to Nena Holguin and to Frances, my wife, whose encouragement through a confusion of climbs was deeply appreciated.

I must also thank Messrs Kaye & Ward for permission to quote from *The Seventh Grade* and *The Challenge*, both by Reinhold Messner, and the *Observer* for permission to quote from a review by Clive James of *Everest Unmasked*.

R.F.

CONTENTS

LIST OF ILLUSTRATIONS

The route up Aconcagua
Strong wind on Makalu
Rawalpindi with Peter Habeler en route to Hidden Peak, 1975
Habeler and seracs on Hidden Peak
With Uschi and the dogs just after divorce, 1977

Following page 152
Training at Villnöss (*photo Volker Corell*)
The house at Villnöss: training among the prayer-flags (*photo Ronald Faux*)
Messner's house at Villnöss (*photo Ronald Faux*)
The view down the valley from the house (*photo Ronald Faux*)
View across the meadow to Messner's cabin (*photo Ronald Faux*)
The cabin that he built unaided (*photo Ronald Faux*)
At K2 Base Camp — the mountain in the background (*copyright John Cleare/Mountain Camera*)
Messner and Habeler after their "oxygen-free" ascent of Everest in 1978 (*photo Ingeborg Scherübel*)
Wolfgang Nairz, leader of the 1978 Austrian Everest expedition
Everest showing the South Col, 1978
1978 Everest expedition: return to Base Camp, snow-blind (*photo Ronald Faux*)
A warm greeting from Ursula Grether (*photo Ronald Faux*)
Everest from the North
The ruins of the Rongbuk monastery on the northern approaches to Everest, 1980
Nena Holguin boarding the aircraft for China
Alone at the summit of Everest

Unacknowledged photographs are the property of Reinhold Messner and the Messner family.

MAPS

INTRODUCTION

by *Reinhold Messner*

I have been asked many times by friends and publishers to write an autobiography and to tell of those things which over and above mountaineering have filled and torn apart the first 36 years of my life. I considered the idea rather premature, I still felt myself to be not old enough. Life lies neither before nor behind me, I am living now and, apart from that, I had not time to write such a book. But when two years ago Ronnie Faux, an English journalist working for *The Times*, suggested that he should write such a book, I agreed. We had met at the foot of Everest when Ronnie had been sent to cover the expedition on which the first oxygen-free ascent was made. His intention was to write about me and my life and to assess me as a person.

He took the trouble not only to come to the mountain and observe me but also joined in my hectic life during the preparation for expeditions. He stayed with me at my home in Villnöss, at my mountaineering school and met my family and friends. Ronnie has also stayed in my small alpine hut, one of the last oases of peace I can find in this all too hectic Europe.

He also has a great interest in mountains, particularly in Mount Everest which has been, time and again, the goal of British expeditions since 1921. Thus a book has emerged that has many facets, above all the viewpoint of the layman. Ronnie has watched me from Base Camp on Everest, as a journalist and spectator, as a listener on my lecture tours and even in dealings with my business partners.

It is difficult to understand a mountaineer totally. I have tried myself to express my experiences "close to the skin" but always as the person up there: climbing higher metre by metre. Here, someone is looking at my life from the outside, not only at my adventures as a mountaineer but as a person with problems and with inner strife that has shaken me with the force of a storm.

When I read the galley proofs I often smiled to myself and had to admit that he was right in many things. What I had been aware of sub-consciously became rationally clear to me on reading the book. If today I am starting out for Makalu on my fifteenth expedition to an 8,000 metre peak, then it is also for this reason that I am driven to do so, hounded on by myself.

I often question whether this is enthusiasm, compulsion or perhaps the work of Sisyphus driving me time and again to the very highest peaks. So, for me, this biography has been a key to my own understanding, an important contribution to what I do, what I experience and what I am. I think it has been written neither too early nor too late. It is here, now.

Villnöss   R.M.
1981

HIGH AMBITION

Chapter 1

THE QUIET TIGER AND *THE TIMES*

WE COULD SEE them in the distance above base camp, two dots moving through the chaos of the icefall. Beyond them, dwarfing the climbers with its huge bulk, rose the western shoulder of Everest in a black shawl of shattered rock layered with yet more ice. Through the glasses the two figures came into closer view, threading their way between twisted seracs, hummocked ice and the dark scars of crevasses.

The news that Reinhold Messner and Peter Habeler had made a ''free'' ascent of Everest under their own steam, without using bottled oxygen, had already come crackling over the radio from one of the higher camps. It was a great achievement, confounding the pessimism of eminent scientists and setting an important standard in Himalayan climbing. The news ''We made it'' was greeted with great excitement, ending hours of uncertainty about the fate of the two climbers.

Carefully they crossed the metal ladders bridging the widest breaches in the ice. Very carefully; for Messner was snow-blind, his eyes painfully inflamed. It would be ironic to have an accident after surviving the rarefied dangers of the final assault, yet many climbers had died there in the two-mile crush of frozen debris that tumbled in infinitely slow motion from the Western Cwm.

The figures resolved into two men in brightly-coloured climbing suits carrying light rucksacks and moving close together. They reached the point where the angle of the slope eased and the glacier ice became mixed with grey moraine. Then they were scrambling up the moraine itself to base camp and being led through the triumphal arch improvised from marker fronds and bunting, grinning ecstatically but with the dark marks of cold and exposure pinched into their faces.

They had proved a point, even if it was perhaps an academic point of massive irrelevance when set against the scale of the risks involved. Messner and Habeler had shown that human beings could reach the highest point of earth unaided. Every previous ascent of Everest had relied on oxygen carried on the climber's back and fed to the lungs through a face mask. The man in the street surviving through a haze of diesel fumes might well say: "So what?" But for mountaineers an old argument had been settled.

Had the summit of Everest been a hundred metres *lower* and yet still the highest point then most probably the question would have been settled 50 years previously by such pioneering stalwarts as Mallory, Norton, Odell and Irvine. Although they had used a cumbersome oxygen supply in the 1924 attempt, the clear feeling among the pioneers was that an unassisted climb would be the more proper and decent thing.

Had the summit been substantially *higher* then the possibility of reaching it without the artificial aid of oxygen would have been positively out of the question. The tantalising fact was that 8,848 metres lay just beyond normal reach, an irresistible challenge to mountaineers; it was a climbing goal of ascetic purity, a physical achievement equal to a new Olympic record and a philosophical point that had to be proved.

What began to intrigue me as a journalist waiting in the discomfort of Everest base camp for this high level conundrum to be resolved was the nature of a man who made his living only a crampon-point away from a lonely and violent death and who pushed both himself and the art of climbing to greater and greater extremes. I began to find Reinhold Messner more absorbing even than Everest because he had achieved so much, climbing more than 2,000 serious routes in the Alps, Himalayas and Andes. Moreover he had tackled some of the most difficult ones entirely on his own. He had been on more than 20 expeditions, to all but the Antarctic continent, and had written more than a dozen books about his exploits. He had the status of a national hero in Germany and Italy, and was a best-selling author, but at the same time led a private life stormy enough to be of continual interest to both the serious and the scurrilous Continental press.

We had met first in London at a lunch organised by Harlech Television Wales, who were to make a film of the Everest attempt. Messner outlined his plans to the executives from HTV and *The Times*, a newspaper which has almost a proprietorial interest in stories about Everest. It had been involved in many of the early expeditions and had a correspondent on the successful ascent in 1953 by Hillary and Tensing. In 1976 I had been to the mountain to write about the British Army's expedition via the South Col route, and here I was again being assigned as *The Times* correspondent on another, even more ambitious attempt. Had I felt persecuted, I might have become suspicious of this persistent tendency to dispatch me to one of the more dangerous places on earth.

Messner explained that he and Peter Habeler, a ski instructor from Mayerhofen in Austria with whom he had made several spectacular climbs, intended quite simply to climb Everest by a new direct route. They would do this by joining an Austrian expedition that was attempting the South Col route and then striking out on their own for the summit. The Austrians would use oxygen. Messner and Habeler would not.

This ambitious statement, made in a London boardroom as the port circulated after an excellent lunch, was hard to associate with that air-starved world of the high Himalayas. Messner himself was receiving some beady scrutiny from a few well-wined sceptics around the table. Did he *look* like a man who could scale Everest in a way no one had ever conquered the mountain before? Frankly, no. Not, that is, if you had the British vision of what a tough adventurer should look like in your mind's eye: all beef and muscle, with bellows lungs and arms like a blacksmith's. This man was lean and lanky. True, the face that appeared beneath a dark thatch of hair had a formidably determined and confident look about it but one *Times* executive observed: "Pleasant chap, but he looks as if a gust of wind would blow him over." As a "tiger" of the climbing world, this one seemed very amiable and quiet-mannered.

Messner was used to having people give him calculating glances, rather in the way that he might have been scrutinised as a newly enrolled gladiator. He knew that bulk and raw brawn were not necessarily an asset on a high mountain and that fitness and experience were more important. He had already scaled three peaks over 8,000 metres without oxygen and had built up an unequalled reputation for the speed of his Alpine ascents. He and Habeler had climbed the Eiger north face in the phenomenally short time of ten hours. The partnership, developed over the years, had reached a perfect intuitive harmony. The plan to climb Everest had been slowly worked towards and was not a new idea.

There were gloomy theories expressed by doctors in Germany that to enter the last elusive metres of Everest without an artificial supply of oxygen would inflict madness on the climber. He would go up with a crazy ambition and come down with a crazy mind. But Messner and Habeler rejected that view as being the modern equivalent of the old notion that if a man travelled at more than ten miles an hour his head would burst.

Messner explained over lunch his keen but sceptical interest in the theories about the physical problems of high altitude climbing, balancing them against the reality of what he had already accomplished. Nanga

Parbat, Manaslu and Hidden Peak — the latter with Habeler, and all of them 8,000 metre mountains climbed without oxygen. The idea, first discussed with Dr Oswald Ölz and Wolfgang Nairz, had fermented quietly for five years until the plan for an Alpine-style attempt, swift and lightweight, had matured logically.

"It is not important for me just to climb Everest, but it is a much greater achievement to climb the mountain without using oxygen. I can sit in my home in Italy and know I can climb Everest with a can of oxygen. Without is an unknown question. Man can reach the moon with the aid of technology but it is a philosophical question to reach the top of Everest without it."

To improve the odds in their favour, compared with those of the early explorers, they had the benefits of modern equipment design — down-filled clothing, triple thickness boots, a final assault tent weighing only one kilo, even an ultra-lightweight rope, all factors that could ensure warmth and speed.

"It is necessary to move quickly," said Messner. "Three days from the Western Cwm is the most we can afford for making it to the top and back. After that the doctors are right. The body deteriorates too quickly." This deterioration takes a ferocious form. Shrinking brain cells, starved of oxygen; bursting blood vessels; vulnerability to exposure; a sharp drop in physical performance. It had to be done in three days or not at all which meant that chance, too, had to be on the climbers' side. The conditions would have to be good, the two men perfectly acclimatised, fit and in the right position to make the attempt. Messner put the likelihood of these critical factors occurring together at no more than 50 per cent.

Looking across the table Messner explained that perhaps the important approach was in the mind. He had climbed three of the highest mountains without distress and without oxygen. He had attempted others and turned back because it was too dangerous. It was not "intelligent" to take risks beyond a certain point. "If I reach only a hundred metres from the top of Everest and cannot go on I shall know it is not possible for me and that will be proved," he said. Messner would not then attempt the top with oxygen, simply because he would not be carrying it. There was no point in suffering the weight of the equipment without having the advantage. He would not be using technology as a hoist. He would go to the top of the mountain; not artificially lower the top of the mountain to him.

From that first meeting over lunch came the firm impression of a singularly determined man who was prepared to risk a great deal to reach this ultimate goal, but who clearly recognised the border between a justifiable and a hare-brained risk. For the last 25 years in Britain there had been immense pride in Hillary and Tensing's first ascent of Everest using oxygen, and the pride in that achievement, which was born of logistics and teamwork, would never wane. Yet, in a way that we all recognised in our hearts, this proposal of Messner's reverted to the feelings of early Alpine Club members who, without knowing anything then of the problems involved, had ruled out oxygen on the grounds that using it would not be fair play.

Back in Scotland, where I was *The Times* correspondent, the political scene was boiling towards the critical Glasgow Garscadden by-election, but in an odd way the campaigning among dingy Clydeside tenements, the political slanging matches and the drone of politicians seemed much less part of the real world than what was happening thousands of miles away in the Himalayas.

As the campaign wore on I was quietly giving Messner a better chance of reaching the top of Everest than the SNP candidate of winning a seat at Westminster. The candidate was a pacifist pro-abortionist in a Catholic area which relied on the arms industry for most of its jobs. Messner was by contrast a man perfectly fitted and prepared for the job he had set his mind on. Then confirmation of the invitation came for me to join the expedition and within three days I was on a Pan Am flight heading east. I handed my valedictory piece on Garscadden to an air hostess who promised to post it in Bahrein and then turned my thoughts entirely towards Everest and the adventurous life of Reinhold Messner.

The Austrians had been at work for some weeks before I was able to reach them. It was a strong and a friendly expedition, the first that the Austrian Alpine Club had ever sent to Everest although Austrian mountaineers had a formidable record elsewhere in the Himalayas. Messner and Habeler grafted themselves on to the team without problems, doing more than their share of the route-finding and establishing camps on the way through the icefall, into the Western Cwm and up the Lhotse face to the South Col. The work of transporting loads and establishing fixed ropes for the Sherpas and sahibs was well under way by the time I flew into Lukla, and the bush telegraph was as ever improving upon the truth.

Sherpa Kham Tsering met me at the spectacular air strip where the flights from Kathmandu sidle in to land in the still early morning air. He cheerfully picked up my huge rucksack and after an hour's steady plodding up the Dudh Kosi valley we rested on a wall to watch a golden eagle circling lazily in the Himalayan sky.

"You go Everest?" Kham Tsering inquired, casually.

"That's correct," I replied.

"But they climb Everest yesterday," he said.

Kham Tsering had been privy to a forked stick that had passed earlier that morning. "It is the Germans. Snow very good, very fast."

"The Austrians, you mean?" I prompted.

"Yes, that's right, the Australians!"

My heart sank into my double boots. I could only hope that Kham Tsering had misread the message or was conforming to the well-intentioned Sherpa habit of telling the visitor what he thought the visitor would best like to hear. If it was true then the expedition had beaten the record by about ten days and was weeks ahead of normal progress towards the summit. At that rate I should arrive at base camp, still some 70 kilometres' walk away to the north, just as the final tent-peg was being drawn and the last Austrian was departing down the Khumbu glacier with a triumphant yodel.

I grew more anxious and at Sangboche airfield was happy to be offered a flight over the Everest area. That would at least allow me to jump ahead and check exactly where the climbers were. It was a flight that Messner had taken a year earlier, and had horrified the pilot by refusing to wear an oxygen mask as the plane clawed its way towards 8,800 metres. He wanted to prove to himself that he was well enough acclimatised to make do with the little bit of oxygen there was in the air.

The pilot, Emil Wick, was a short, powerfully built Swiss who had to sit on a cushion in order to see over the instrument panel and out along the tapering snout of his Pilatus Porter. He was the only pilot qualified to fly into what he called "The Hole", the narrow valley formed by the massive walls of Lhotse, Nuptse and Everest. He was highly experienced, trained in the Swiss Alps and had moved on to bigger things; he spoke with a Euro-American drawl.

"That's right, I remember that Messner guy," he said. "There I was flying along and I took a look round, checking that all the oxygen indicators were bobbing up and down showing that everyone was surviving nicely, when I see him sitting there with his mask in his lap. I made some urgent kind of sign to let him know that he's likely to keel over and die but he just smiles at me. I assume he's got some kind of gills. He looked a bit blue but he didn't keel over."

Messner had coped well with that sudden reduction of oxygen caused when the plane took off and climbed rapidly to more than 10,000 metres. It was a good test and a useful reconnaissance of the route he planned to do. Setting out to follow his flight path some time later the Porter bounced down the Sangboche runway, the highest landing strip in the world, leaving a brown swirl of dust. It was hardly airborne when the end of the runway slipped beneath the undercarriage and the light aircraft drifted over a deep chasm and banked steeply to avoid crashing into the mountain wall on the opposite side of the valley. The Porter's nose contains one of the Rolls Royce turbo-prop engines of a type which powered the Viscount airliner and is ideal for operating in the thin Himalayan air. Nevertheless we had to claw for height in wide, slow circles watching the incredible panorama slip by. Ama Dablam, now an entirely different shape, was baulking a bank of thick cloud and projecting it skywards. On the edge of the circle lay Kangchenjunga, Makalu and, beyond the complex south face of Nuptse, the black triangular cape of the goddess-mountain Chomolungma which Westerners know as Everest.

The aircraft made a slow climbing turn towards the ridge that falls in massive broken steps into the Khumbu glacier. The flank of the mountain rushed towards us, slid beneath the wheels and plunged away, a straight drop of 2,600 metres. The Western Cwm opened up and the nose edged into it, tracking now the north face of Nuptse. The lip of the ridge was just below us and looked impossible to traverse, with huge cornices, formed by the tearing wind, overhanging the steep drop — fluted walls of ice impermanently poised.

Directly ahead the fortress top of Lhotse swung into view. The sensation was that we were still and the mountains were swerving around us, until the plane hit a jetstream of turbulence. A highway of invisible cobbles shook the wings and vibrated the windows. The pilot thrust the control column forward.

"I'm winding the bastard down. Can't get any higher, no good," he explained.

The controls were obviously leaden in the thin air and the plane needed plenty of speed to remain manoeuvrable. The south-west face of Everest spun past a hundred metres away. The cliff that had proved impassable to at least five expeditions looked forbidding and the winter winds had stripped all the loose covering from the snowfield above the rocks. The south-west face was certainly not a possibility for Messner. Even less so was the long imposing pillar of rock running from the cwm directly towards the south summit. It appeared a fine direct line, no doubt, but was varnished with a thin, treacherous film of verglas.

In the desolate hollow of the South Col there was no sign of life. I could see some tattered remnants littered around from previous expeditions but no new tents. The summit ridge looked empty too, although the vast scale of Everest's final pyramid would easily obliterate anything so insignificant as two climbers.

Flattening its dive, the plane made a long descending curve into the Western Cwm. There the Austrians were, one party plodding up the Lhotse Face towards the Geneva Spur, moving very slowly, occasionally stopping altogether and leaning on the ski sticks that they carried for support. Some of them were using oxygen. I could see the masks facing up to us little more than 30 metres below, a rope of four climbers with another group following about 150 metres lower.

We were now in a straight shallow dive with the walls of Everest and Nuptse closed in above us. The sky was perfectly clear and the valley brilliant with sunshine. At Camp II climbers waved as the plane descended smoothly towards the edge of the icefall, cutting through the still air of the Western Cwm. In one tobogganing dive we pitched over the edge of the 600 metre drop where the high glacier of the cwm is cut into massive slices and begins its slow tumble to the valley. In less than a minute, base camp was pivoting on the port wing tip. There were no jubilant flags flying. We could spot loads being moved up in convoy through the icefall. There was every sign that the expedition was still busily at work. Even though it might take me three or four days to reach the base camp from Sangboche, I should still be in time to catch Messner and Habeler before the summit attempt.

Chapter 2

UNMASKING EVEREST

MESSNER WATCHED THE Pilatus Porter cruising down the Western Cwm, its engine throttled back to a whisper. It was out of place in this wilderness, an intrusive aerial grandstand, swooping down to peer at people in their private world of isolation and fear. For those were his realities, the subjective dangers of high mountain climbing. There were also the other dangers of avalanche, storm and exhaustion caused by living too long at high altitude and beyond these the ludicrous damage that could be inflicted by a bad sardine. Peter had eaten one such the previous day at Camp III and was now laid low, clutching his stomach and complaining that whatever went in one end was violently evacuated at the other. Was the grand plan, the ultimate climb, to be jeopardised by a single sardine?

Messner had departed from the small encampment on the Lhotse face early that day with two Sherpas, Mingma and Ang Dorje, leaving Peter behind ill and upset in his sleeping bag. The weather was perfect. Above him on the South Col and around the castellated summit of Lhotse shreds of spindrift marked the presence of a wind much higher up the mountain. But at the moment the steeply-angled boiler-plate ice of the Lhotse face stretched gleaming ahead, catching the light in a million smaller sparkles. He felt boundingly fit and moved with an easy, swift rhythm well ahead of the two Sherpas.

The idea of making a solo attempt on Everest without oxygen had already formed in his mind. Even if Peter had been with him the two would be moving separately, unroped. It could be argued that in a fast, alpine-style attempt on such a ridge he would have more chance of success alone than with a partner. The south-west ridge was not technically difficult, just unbelievably long. Climbing with a partner certainly helped morale but could be a liability if one of them slipped when they were roped together. The greatest dream would be to stand alone on the highest point of the world after arriving there without trickery, without

21

any artificial help. That really would stun the world, that really would be the ultimate climb.

The ambition to make a solo bid was burning strongly in him when the three men pitched their camp in the desolate hollow of the South Col. Around them lay the remains of other expeditions: tent frames bent and twisted, oxygen bottles discarded and empty, left by a long line of mountaineers trying to suckle a bit of comfort in that awesome place. The desire for comfort was great as they looked into space at the curve of the earth spiked by the summits of the highest mountains that men would ever see.

Mingma took to his sleeping bag immediately the tent was erected. Most Sherpas have a remarkable tolerance of the effects of altitude up to more than 7,000 metres but beyond that even they feel the choking thinness of the air. Their culture also teaches them that the mountains are the home of unforgiving gods. Why risk offending them? What was the point of climbing to the summits? Life was difficult enough anyway: a hard material struggle of scratching crops out of thin soil and earning enough to survive. Already one Sherpa had died in the icefall, crushed and buried. It was beyond their understanding that these obviously wealthy foreigners should come to this remote land and risk, or even lose, their lives scrambling to the tops of mountains. It was true that for the Sherpas there were material riches to be had in carrying loads for these strangers. It was good to be paid for doing something which was normally a necessary unpaid task. But the reasons for this windfall were dubious even to some of those Sherpas who had reached the highest summits in the world and who were revered for their bravery.

The storm came like a physical blow, a distant ravenous howl growing in intensity and then suddenly shaking the tent with a terrible violence.

Mingma sank deeper in his sleeping bag as the first onslaught of the ice particles picked up by the wind was hurled at them across the Col. Ang Dorje kept one hand on the wildly shaking tent frame, the other steadying the stove on which Messner was trying to cook. It was a lukewarm meal, followed by a sleepless night spent hanging on to the tent to prevent it from being carried away. The wind ripped and tore at them forcing fine powder ice through the seams, covering everything with freezing spindrift that penetrated everywhere. By morning the three were exhausted. Mingma lay motionless, fatalistically prepared to accept death and exhausted beyond the point of fear by cold and lack of oxygen.

The tent was torn and chaotic. There was no oxygen to revive Mingma — a part of Messner's insistence on a ''pure'' ascent. He and Ang Dorje tried to put up an emergency tent in the slight lulls but each time the wind returned fiercely, drowning speech and filling the air with blinding snow that left a rime of ice over their faces. The "death zone" was living up to its reputation. The second, smaller tent was eventually erected as a shaky but improved shelter and the three men huddled in it waiting for the wind to abate. It was impossible to attempt a retreat down the Lhotse face even though Messner had become very concerned about the condition of the two Sherpas. The first signs of frostbite were appearing on his own face and fingertips and the thought of a solo climb to the summit had become a senseless dream, an idea blown into oblivion by the reality of the storm.

Night returned colder and wilder than ever. Outside, the sky remained an unrelenting grey, the wind howled at more than 150 miles an hour and the temperature had dropped to minus 50 degrees. When he checked the tent poles, Messner's fingers stuck to the metal.

Over the radio, Camp II reported that the forecast for the following day predicted an improvement in the weather. The radio link cheered him, a reassuring voice coming through the static, inquiring anxiously about conditions on the South Col and how they were surviving.

The act of lying there with the wind tearing at the tent, knowing that in the thin air their bodies were actually dying around them for lack of oxygen, demanded a tremendous effort: not to panic, not to give in to a hysterical fear. What would happen if one of the Sherpas cracked or went mad? The answer was relayed from the doctors at Base Camp: give no drugs, thump him if necessary. Marvellous, a punch-up in a rickety tent on the South Col — that would probably end them all.

The hurricane screamed all night, but as the first pale light appeared its force relented. Messner shook the two Sherpas. Mingma slowly came to but immediately he realised which side of the grave he had woken on he was filled with a powerful urge to leave the South Col.

The two set off on the descent, leaving Messner to collapse the tent and weight it down out of the wind with old oxygen cylinders. The storm might have relented but a strong wind was now blowing from the south directly on to the Lhotse face. Slowly Messner descended towards the rocks of the Geneva Spur, searching for signs of the two Sherpas who should have been waiting for him but had flown. He shouted their names but there was no reply and it was not until he climbed through the cloud that he saw them far below heading down the Lhotse face, not looking back at all.

The storm had torn at the mountain and the fragile path the climbers had made on it. Everest never relented. In the icefall a ladder spanning a crevasse collapsed as he was half way across it, leaving him hanging by one hand from the safety rope. A surge of determination to survive shocked him and overrode the exhaustion and despair of the last two days. He clawed his way to the edge of the crevasse and safety.

He arrived at Base Camp completely drained and with his experience of the South Col written in hard lines on his face. He had aged; his eyes were hollowed and dark with tiredness, his skin pinched and raw from the cold wind, his resolve drained by the altitude. It was some time before the bad memories were erased and the old ideals began to seep back, helped by calm days and rest which allowed the shreds of resolve to regroup and rally for another try. A number of Sherpas later complained to the government about Messner's bullying attitude and his claims. It was the "bullying" that probably saved their lives.

The storm that had gripped Everest gave way to a spell of calm. The Western Cwm, with its gigantic walls of ice grained with grey rock, returned to a cathedral quiet. The mornings were still. The slant of the sunlight descending slowly on the face of Nuptse reflected with a fierce brightness. The temperature went from freezing cold to uncomfortable heat. Habeler also returned to base as three of the Austrians put the calm weather to good use and moved up from the South Col. On 3 May, Wolfgang Nairz, the expedition leader, Horst Bergmann, Robert Schauer and Ang Phu, the sirdar, reached the summit using oxygen.

The rhythm of the expedition was re-established. Stores continued to flow through the icefall to the higher camps and morale grew again. Then three more Austrians left for the South Col but were prevented from reaching even that point by waist-deep fresh snow lying on the Lhotse face.

At Camp II Habeler joined up with Robert Schauer, a medical student from Graz who already had a reputation for climbing hard routes. Habeler saw the lean, lanky figure of the young Austrian in the communal tent staring reflectively into a bowl of hot soup.

"How did it go?" Habeler inquired.

"Fine, but I don't envy you your attempt."

"Why's that? Why do you say that?"

"Well, I gave it a try without oxygen for a while near the South Summit. I took my mask off and climbed but it was terrible. I was absolutely gasping for air and all my strength went into that simple effort. There was nothing left over for climbing. I tell you, Peter, I don't see how anyone could climb to the top without oxygen."

Robert was very emphatic and that impressed Peter. He had seen

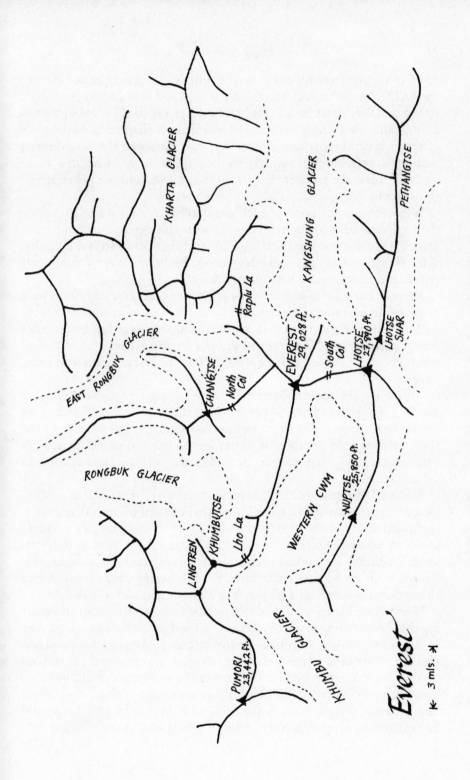

KHARTA GLACIER

KANGSHUNG GLACIER

PETHANGTSE

Raplu La

EAST RONGBUK GLACIER

CHANGTSE

North Col

EVEREST 29,028 ft.

South Col

LHOTSE 27,890 ft.

LHOTSE SHAR

RONGBUK GLACIER

KHUMBUTSE

Lho La

WESTERN CWM

NUPTSE 25,850 ft.

LINGTREN

PUMORI 23,442 ft.

KHUMBU GLACIER

Everest

← 3 mls. ↗

Reinhold return from his ordeal on the South Col looking like an old man.
He had felt so ill himself on the Lhotse face and now Robert Schauer, a
strong and very determined climber, had actually tried to make progress
at high altitude without oxygen and had almost collapsed from the mere
effort of breathing. It was all very well talking about climbing Everest
without oxygen when it was a theoretical question discussed in a warm
room. It was quite another thing to sit in the cold shadow of Everest and
think about it.

What was the real point of such an attempt? Wasn't it really no more
than splitting hairs to reach the summit without oxygen? Surely the act of
reaching the summit was the thing? What if the doctors were right, what
if the shortage of oxygen really did damage his brain? Wasn't this grossly
selfish and irresponsible towards his family?

Messner knew his friend well enough to see that these questions were
revolving in his mind. Peter had the hang-dog look of an anxious blood-
hound. His doubt was instilled not by a lack of courage but by evidence
which appeared to condemn the whole exercise. He was not surprised
when Peter announced that he would prefer to make an attempt using
oxygen.

"I'm sorry, Reinhold," Peter said, "but I do not feel good about going
on. The risk is too much. What happens if one of us collapses and we
do not have oxygen? The other will not have the strength to help. By the
time anyone could get there it would be too late; he would be dead or
brain-damaged." The oxygen-free idea was wild, ill-conceived and
unjustifiable.

Reinhold repeated that he had no wish to go to the summit using oxygen, and it was curious how the Austrians accepted his tacit dismissal of
their own achievement without any ill-will. How could they be polite to
someone who plainly believed they had "lowered the summit to themselves" rather than climbed to the top? Few mountaineers could make it
clear to someone who had just climbed Everest using oxygen that he had
cheated and still remain a friend. Yet Messner had said just that.

When Peter Habeler called down to base camp on the radio announcing that he was going to use oxygen after all and asking for another partner
to join him, he was surprised by the response. Among the Austrians
waiting at the foot of the icefall were several who resented his sudden
appearance as competition for themselves in a conventional summit bid.
Some shrewd calculations had been made about the levels of stores at the
higher camps and particularly the number of oxygen bottles that would
be available to support further attempts. Peter was furious at being told

that if he wanted to change his plans then he must join the end of the queue.

His fury was quickly translated into action. His doubts dissolved in white rage and Messner saw the look of determination return to his partner's face. He knew immediately that he would not be attempting the summit on his own. Messner was glad. There was no one whose judgement on a mountain he respected more, no one who was fitter or better prepared to make the attempt.

Peter turned to him sheepishly and said: "Well, Reinhold, it seems that it is the two of us again."

"We will do it, Peter. We will be all right," was the reply.

By May 7 the two men were climbing together again from Camp III on the Lhotse face towards the Yellow Band and the rocks above the Geneva Spur. They moved quickly and Messner sank into the limbo of rhythmic concentration, his mind shifting uneasily between the relentless effort of planting one foot higher than the last and an overwhelming sense of futility. Mountaineering was a joke, a very serious joke.

The two climbers reached the South Col and settled into their small tent. Outside, the sunset coloured the fantastic array of peaks. They could clearly see the neighbouring summits of Lhotse and Nuptse, the flat top of Pumori now well dwarfed below them and, out beyond the velvet dark valleys, the high pyramid of Makalu.

The three Sherpas had departed and base camp radioed to give a good forecast for the following day's weather. Both men felt an overwhelming sense of reassurance. The long shoulder of Everest led up from the Col, with its conventional pattern of ridges and gullies choked with snow. There was nothing technically hard to catch their eye, nothing to compare with the difficulties that both climbers had overcome in the past. Their gaze was one of quick and skilful assimilation based on years of staring at mountain faces; working out the best line, measuring the angle, judging the condition of the snow, the quality of the rock.

As they prepared themselves for the night, Eric Jones, the Welsh climber and photographer, arrived on the South Col having toiled up the Lhotse face to film the attempt. He moved into the tent next to the others and settled down in his sleeping bag exhausted by the long climb.

Messner and Habeler discussed their chances as the wind stirred with a long moan across the Col. The ice stiffening the foot of the tent remained untouched by the roaring stove.

Messner was confident that they were as physically and mentally prepared for the attempt as they would ever be. Everything depended on the condition of the mountain. They had climbed well that day, moving up the Lhotse face and across to the Geneva Spur in fine style, climbing quickly in spite of the deep layer of fresh snow. Both felt that with luck they would reach the South Summit; with real luck they would make the top.

Messner lay in his sleeping bag feeling the cold creep through the layers of down. Beside him Peter stirred, curling himself into a tighter, warmer ball. Outside, the wind across the col sounded peaceful compared to the fury during Messner's previous night in the same place. The hours dragged by. There was little chance of real sleep. Both men were too keyed up by the challenge the day would bring. Now was the time for doubt to crawl into the mind. Were the pessimistic doctors right? Was it really worth such a risk? What if the brain cells really did die?

Messner, in the dim light filtering through the tent walls, considered the still form next to him. Peter had been through so many other adventures with him, but this was different. The ordinary dangers of climbing held little fear for either of them. Both were perfectly capable of handling the technical matter of moving over steep ice or rock. Years of mountaineering together had bred a strong trust and respect. But the extremes and unknowns of Everest were so different. The finest human machinery could not function without the fuel of oxygen and on a mountain of the scale of Everest they would become weak and vulnerable. It was one thing to think up an attempt in the comfort of home to convince yourself that a particular climb was possible in theory, but quite another thing to be actually on the mountain and trying to pick the way along an untrodden pathway that wavered between success and the grave.

At 3 a.m. on May 8 Messner stirred, reaching out for the still frozen lump of snow they had collected the night before and breaking pieces of it into the billy for a brew. The roar of the stove woke Peter and the two men struggled into frost-stiffened climbing gear inside their sleeping bags. They took turns to drink the lukewarm potion that Messner had produced. By 5 a.m. they were ready.

They had on silk underwear and a fleecy underlayer beneath a one-piece down suit. Double-layered clip-sided boots were protected by insulated neoprene gaiters. Three pairs of gloves, two hats and goggles completed the kit. They carried 20 metres of lightweight rope between them, crampons and a light ice axe each.

Inside the tent, hoar-frost crumbled from the tent roof as they moved. Outside, their hearts sank. The cold was bitter at first light. The South Col was deep in fresh snow and a biting wind blew from the west sending up chill swirls of spindrift. The valley below was clogged with thick cloud and the sky darkly overcast. The conditions did not look possible but the two men were determined to look at the start of the ridge. They shouted their intentions to Eric Jones who took one glance from his tent and dismissed the attempt as hopeless.

Before 6 a.m. they were moving across the Col towards the ridge. Neither said a word, concentrating on the immediate demands of drawing breath and developing the essential rhythm. Messner sensed that Habeler felt even less at ease than himself about the weather, perhaps because it made the margin between a good decision and a lethal one too narrow, especially since he had a wife and child to consider. Messner felt alone. Bitterly he reflected that there was no one who was totally dependent on him. Sometimes that had advantages but not when the bleak Himalayan wind howled around him. It would be a comfort to believe that someone did deeply care, but could he expect that? People tended to consider him somehow invulnerable after he had survived so many adventures, after years when danger had become more or less a background to his daily life. Yet beneath the mountaineer was an ordinary man with ordinary problems.

A sleet squall tore at them from the edge of the ridge. Peter nodded towards the rocks beside the gully which formed the normal route and which was choked with fresh snow. They moved across and on the firmer surface their progress speeded up but conditions remained marginal. A strip of brightness in the sky had disappeared and over Makalu to the east snow was falling heavily. Peter scratched an arrow in the snow pointing downwards. Reinhold interpreted this as a wish to return to the South Col and he cut another arrow pointing upwards. In fact Peter argued later that he had intended his arrow as a marker to make route-finding easier on the return.

Within four hours the two men reached the site of the final camp on the South Ridge, level with the summit of Lhotse which rose on the far side of the South Col in a huge broken arête. The tent had been left there by the first summit party.

Messner registered a few thoughts on a small tape recorder as they waited for the stove to melt a panful of snow in the shelter of the high camp. ''Eight thousand five hundred metres and the last camp. We have arrived here quite quickly considering the conditions. The weather is extremely bad and our chances of reaching the top must be in the balance but we both feel okay.''

Deep fresh snow would make trail-breaking onward extremely arduous but both men were in good spirits although weakened by the lack of oxygen. They knew that if they failed now and retreated to the South Col, driven down by the ice-laden wind or the chance of avalanche, there would be no hope of attempting the summit. They would have neither the time nor the strength to drag themselves back into this position before the real storms of the monsoon arrived, and other climbers on the Austrian expedition would want to make their own attempts. Messner felt strong and he could see in Peter's face a reflection of his own determination. They would try at least to reach the South Summit, some four hours away, and see how things looked from there.

Cautiously they dropped into the hollow below the South Summit, aware of the huge cornices built there by the wind. The ridge began to incline upwards again and was blocked by a steep pitch of rock and ice. Vaguely, Messner registered that this must be the Hillary Step, the last obstacle before the summit. He uncoiled the 20-metre length of rope, clipped one end into his harness and handed the other to Peter. Then like an automaton he began cutting his way up the ice pitch. After every few swipes of the axe he paused, mouth gaping and lungs straining for air. At the top of the pitch he turned and pulled out the ciné camera he had been keeping warm inside his down suit. The frames clattered through as Peter dragged himself up the pitch, keenly aware that on one side lay a 2,500 metre drop into Nepal and on the other a similar plunge into Tibet. The "ladder" he was climbing had fragile, crumbling rungs.

The two climbers turned for the last section of the ridge, taking the lead alternately. Reinhold watched Peter leaning into the slope, the wind blurring his outline. He could see the bright blue of his jacket, his head bending over the shaft of the ice axe which he had driven deep into the snow as he stopped, gasping for the breath with which to make the next few lung-racking steps. Then the rope jerked tight and Messner moved forward passing Habeler.

Now he could see his face parchment brown and tight with cold; his eyes hidden by snow-goggles which had a rim of ice around the edges. But not a word was exchanged. Their partnership had rarely worked better. They climbed automatically, no longer aware that they were approaching the summit of Everest and that they would be the first human beings to reach it "purely". Another kind of purity had been attained, a trance-like state of physical effort.

Messner moved upwards, plunging the shaft of his ice axe into the snow surface, sometimes pulling on it with both hands, and all the time reaching for air. There was not enough breath for talk. Every gasp must be drawn into the lungs and converted into action. One more blow with the axe. One more pull from the shoulders. Another cramponned boot lifted and kicked into the hard surface. Twenty-nine thousand feet beneath them, another twenty-eight to go.

Now Messner felt curiously relaxed. His movements had a slow dream-like quality. He was vaguely aware of strange electronic music bursting through his mind. There was now nothing higher; they were perched upon the brow from which that terrible mane of wind-borne ice streamed over towards Tibet. A few more strenuous kicks and then the angle eased. The core of his mind felt numbed but his body reached out for that final, ultimate point. A raw wind with nothing to stop or deflect it hammered through their bodies and into that magnificent pure emptiness suddenly obtruded a metal tripod: an incongruous, man-made thing ground clean of paint by the abrasive cold, the finishing post for the most dramatic of all contests.

They reached the tripod and sank to the ground, legs dangling over the drop into China, the torment of climbing over, the dream realised.

He stood alone on the top of Everest with the wind howling around him, whipping the snow from the summit ridge and turning it into a wild swirl of freezing dust. Peter had already set off down. He was anxious because his arms were beginning unaccountably to feel stiff. For a few minutes Messner savoured the ultimate loneliness of standing on the world's highest point and then set off too. Peter's tracks were already disappearing as the wind combed over the surface of the snow. At the Hillary Step he lowered himself gingerly over the steep edge and descended to the hollow below the South Summit. Immediately the slope tilted upwards ahead of him he felt a colossal drain of energy. He was soon gasping for breath, leaden-legged and resting every few steps, his lungs working over-time in the thin air.

On the South Summit there was no sign of Peter. Messner peered into the mist which now reduced visibility to a few hundred yards and tried to pick out the descent route. He started down reassured each time some small recognisable rock feature loomed into view. He could not see Peter but there were signs of his recent passing. A broad groove with a narrow mark running parallel to it showed that Peter had opted for the easier way down the mountain, and had glissaded down the gully. What a place! The gully disappeared over the precipice of the Kanshung face — 2,500 metres directly into China.

Messner was so confident of his companion's ability it did not occur to him that he could now have an accident. More marks on the mountain showed where Peter had traversed towards the camp on the south summit ridge and found another gully to glissade down.

Visibility was really poor now and Messner had continually to lift his snow goggles to pick out the route. He descended at a more stately pace, digging his heels into the slope and moving clumsily but surely down to the South Col.

He descended a band of ice-glazed rocks facing into the slope and then down a gentler slope that bore all the signs of recent avalanche. Then there were the tents of the South Col camp and Eric Jones offering him tea and congratulations. Peter had escaped injury in the avalanche, apart from a bruised ankle and a burst down suit. He had arrived on the South Col in a whirl of snow and feathers in the incredible time of one hour from the summit. A fantastic record.

They contacted the lower camp by radio and gave the news of their victory. They could not yet feel triumphant. Peter was very tired and Messner's eyes were becoming red and painful. Clearly he had left his goggles off for too long in the grey deceptive light. That night on the South Col he rolled around in agony, feeling as if his eyes were covered in burning sand. The next day they descended, Peter leading the way down the Lhotse face, each step taking them closer to Base Camp and fame.

Chapter 3

PROFESSIONAL ARCHITECT OR PROFESSIONAL
MOUNTAINEER?

A SMALL PAIR of hands appeared over the edge of the churchyard wall at St. Peter, Villnöss. The fingers felt the rough texture of the granite block, settled on the deepest indent and gripped hard. The woman tending the gravestones between the wall and the church looked up in surprise. There was a long fall directly into the road on the other side of the wall. What lunatic daredevil was scaling such a drop and undignifying the dead?

A short-cropped head of dark hair appeared over the edge of the wall and a pale face set with very dark and fiercely-determined eyes followed. Then a wiry figure swung on to the wall top, gave a final irreverent heave on the tomb of the Augscholl family and dropped lightly into the graveyard.

"So it's you, Reinhold Messner," she scolded; "imagine climbing such a place, and you the son of the teacher. Away with you!" The old dame checked her wrath. Even at the age of twelve Reinhold Messner already had the reputation for being a child not to tangle with. He had a direct nature. He was a conscientious worker particularly at things he enjoyed doing but was not one meekly to follow the herd or take discipline. He had been known to walk out of church in the middle of Mass and play truant from his own father's school. His temper when roused was fierce. Even his mother admitted that Reinhold's retribution was "extreme". What about that boy who had to be taken to the doctor after the young Messner's righteous wrath had been roused?

The boy grinned back at her partly from impudence but mainly from a feeling of triumph. The churchyard wall was a steep and exposed place. The stone blocks gave just sufficient holds to cling to and there was one smooth block three-quarters of the way up which had halted all the other boys from St. Peter's school who had tried it. Reinhold had reached that place, balanced delicately up and reached for the edge of a higher block. He felt the exhilarating flood of strength surge through his arms as he made the final pull on to the wall top. Triumph, to do what no one else had done; admiration, or grudging respect, from the boys below who had failed or not even dared to try; and outrage from the old dame. An early demonstration, perhaps, of the rewards of mountaineering.

It was here that Reinhold Messner grew up, in the village of St. Peter in Funes, as the Italians call it; Villnöss as it is known in Austria. His background was therefore that beautiful but politically torn part of Europe, the South Tyrol which has the misfortune to sit on the borders of the two strong but sharply contrasting cultures of Italy and Austria. The 265,500 German-speaking South Tyroleans bid "Willkommen in Südtirol", the 138,000 Italians "Benvenuti in Alto Adige".

Until 1918 the region was part of Austria but under the peace treaty which ended the First World War, the South Tyrol became Italy's 92nd province. When he came to power Mussolini tried ruthlessly to place a positive Italian stamp on the region, the Fascist regime importing "colonising" families from the south of Italy. The moves were deeply resented by the German-speaking Tyroleans and until the late 1960s terrorist acts were carried out which further divided and embittered the two communities. When Italy and Austria signed a new agreement in 1946 Italy retained control over the region but the South Tyrol achieved its own autonomous government. The two cultures co-exist now but not without underlying friction. The terrorist bombing campaign persisted until November 1969 when the Italians worked out a plan with Austria to end the unrest by granting greater autonomy to the region, though they widened the official use of the Italian language and changed the official name of the province from South Tyrol to Alto Adige.

The region is extremely beautiful. More than three-quarters of the total land area lies above 1,000 metres.

Luis Trenker, a local writer, declared that "most of our land seems suspended from our cool skies". South Tyroleans come of hardy stock: self-reliant and candid, shrewd, pious and sensitive. Life in their valleys follows a slow, seasonal rhythm and the pattern in Villnöss is no exception. People there live off the land and their standard of living depends on its being kept well. The fundamentally important things here all relate to wind, rain and sunshine, to avalanches and landslides, to meadows and fields, the age of wood and the fitness of cattle. The values are simple, eternal and anchored firmly to the old faith.

The valley runs at right-angles to the narrow funnel of the Brenner Pass linking Innsbruck in Austria with Bolzano in Italy, a funnel choked with motorways, railways, power lines and industry. Villnöss remains away from this busy international conduit. At its lower end, the valley is broad and threaded by a winding road. The fields lead upwards at a gentle angle beneath slopes covered with pinewoods. In springtime the sun filters through this woodland creating tranquil pools of blue light or falls in bright shafts on the meadows which are already showing the first rash of Alpine flowers. The meadows are neatly cropped and look immaculately groomed. Chalet houses with generous eaves and roofs of bleached shingle dot the hillsides in random orderliness. They look well-settled into the quiet community.

There are two main villages in Villnöss. St. Peter is one of them and is a picturesque ribbon of dwellings built on either side of the road with a spur running up to a high shoulder on which the church stands. Opposite the church, on the first floor of a high building, is the school attended by some 90 to 100 children who come from the farms and hotels in the valley.

Throughout Reinhold's childhood, the Messner family home was a large flat on the top floor of a house near the centre of St. Peter. It lay above a butcher's shop and had a central kitchen where everyone congregated around a scrubbed pinewood table, and a warren of smaller rooms running off a central hallway. Frau Messner kept the place neat and scrupulously clean and the flat always had a welcoming, secure air about it for the Messner children. Outside, a wild grape-vine clambered around the wall of the boundary, the ground behind the house rose steeply towards the church and beyond that lay the high mountains.

Maria and Josef Messner brought up eight sons and one daughter in these cramped but orderly surroundings. Josef was the headmaster of the local school, a short brisk man with a positive cheerful manner. Maria bore their first son, Helmut, in 1943 and regularly produced children over the next fourteen years. She had acquired the quiet patience necessary to bring up such a large family, a plump and thoughtful lady with a long switch of fine hair drawn into a neat bun.

Reinhold was born on September 17, 1944, a year after Helmut; then came Günther, Erich, the one girl Waltraud, Siegfried, Hubert, Hansjorg and finally Werner. The Messners were not an unusually large family by Villnöss standards where the community, almost exclusively Roman Catholic, had a prodigious record of producing babies.

Although Josef and Maria tried not to become involved in the disagreeable Austrian-Italian argument, they did resent strongly the government's Italianisation campaign. German was the family's first language and by nature the Messners were more Austrian than Italian. For that reason, the parents were careful to choose names for their children which could not be Italianised. The result sounded like the cast of a Wagner opera, but at least they were ethnically intact.

Unlike urban Italy, rural communities did not suffer badly during the war and the South Tyrol kept as far as possible from the lunacy that was affecting life outside the valley. Sealed into Villnöss by a world war and difficult post-war years for Italy, the Messner children considered the valley their world. From an early age the peace of the village and the excitement found in the surrounding mountains impressed themselves on Reinhold. Expeditions and holidays into the Geisler Alps were frequent. Each summer, from the age of five, he went with Josef and Maria and his brothers to spend the long holiday in a farm above the valley on a broad pasture directly beneath the Geisler Alps. Although this high place, Gschmagenhart, was only a few kilometres from the family home in St. Peter, it felt entirely different.

The pasture lay above the tree line, a broad swathe of meadow stitched with the brilliant threads of Alpine flowers. The "farm" used by the Messners was a tall building of ancient logs. In traditional Alpine style, the sleeping quarters were on a dark shelf above the living room. Meals were cooked in a shed near by. It was a frugal holiday, but in the crisp, clear days of May and June or in the drowsy warmth of August, the family would not have exchanged it for a palace on the Riviera. They never tired of that beautiful place. Behind the farmhouse the Geisler Alps were set close on the skyline, huge grey teeth of rock, a long line of fine peaks which at that time were little explored. In young Reinhold's mind they became the only mountains in the world, the peaks that guarded the end of the earth. He would watch the sun climb slowly behind them each morning and etch their black symmetry into the sky. He saw them when mist turned their shapes into ghostly giants, when the full blast of summer heat made them look cracked, old and parched and when, with the last lick of colour from the sunset, they turned into a row of flames. They were brilliant, ever-changing and totally enduring objects with their own character and their own strength.

Josef was a keen climber and did not hesitate to introduce his sons to the sport. Reinhold was aged five when he climbed the highest of the Geisler peaks with his father, mother and elder brother Helmut. He recalls being awakened at five o'clock and crawling out of the warm hay in the roof of the hut. Beyond the heavy stable door, the countryside was still and the sky full of stars. He dressed quickly in the cold early light, teeth chattering. His father filled the rucksack with enough food for the day and they watched him putting a coil of hemp rope in as well. That sent a wave of excitement through Reinhold and Helmut. Shortly after, the four of them were crossing the meadow towards the edge of the forest.

Hoar-frost hung on the yellowing grass and the pine trees appeared etched darkly against the pale grey rocks of the mountains. The path dropped down into a shallow valley and a splash of paint on some stones indicated the way out again. The sun was just touching the northern edge of the Furchetta, giving an impression that the Geisler peaks were a gigantic curtain, a dividing wall between two worlds. The air was transparently clear and cold, turning breath to mist. The slightest noise carried a long way so they spoke in whispers, an involuntary action in this quiet place. Josef filled the water bottle from a stream and then joined the others where the path went through a clump of larch trees, zig-zagging up the last patches of grass and a few weather-beaten pines into the slope of scree. The Geisler peaks, now bathed in morning light, excelled in height and promise. At the last stunted tree Josef hid his cigarette tin in a hollow trunk and placed a flat stone on top of it. Climbing up the limestone scree was more energetic than Reinhold had imagined. The stones became finer and the two boys found they had to concentrate on every step. It was easiest to set down the whole of one shoe sole and choose bigger blocks to stand on, moving very evenly. Josef leading the way pointed this out to his boys and they copied his steady, unhurried pace.

In the crook of the col snow was still lying, the grey dead snow left over from spring, and on the other side they saw a series of gullies descending from the Saas Rigais. The path led down past the foot of these gullies in a slope of fine scree. The four climbers, Josef, Maria, Reinhold and Helmut, descended quickly, digging their heels into the surface and "running" down the slope. The stones clattered and surged around their feet.

Now and again there was another sound of stonefall descending from higher up the mountain and Josef explained that this was caused by snow melting the ice that bound the loose material together. The gentle splash of a stream also broke the silence as they prepared for the next section of the climb.

Josef pulled the hemp rope from his rucksack and Reinhold felt excited at the thought that the real climb was about to begin. It was a great feeling of exhilaration. The steep rocky gully rose above them, the walls of yellow rock to left and right overhanging in part. The two boys lost some of their confidence gazing at the steep gully which had blocks in it the size of houses and ice glinting in the corners that were out of the sun. Maria went first, followed by Josef with Helmut and finally Reinhold. The first proper climb. Once they had started it was much easier than he had expected — at each step upwards another hold always materialised and a way through appeared. Then there was always the rope leading tightly up to father who stood watchfully overlooking his two young tyros.

Reinhold forgot about the increasing exposure and thought how each single section of the climb was actually much less difficult in itself than the wall beside the steps of his house. At the steepest points, where the rocks were scraped by the passage of many boots, wire rope had been fixed into the rock providing a secure handrail. There was a feeling of great excitement as he saw the big iron cross on the summit ahead, separated from them by an airy ridge. To the right the wall fell steeply into the valley. On the left the exposure was so great that the boys did not dare glance down. A mountaineer descending towards them observed: "Very exposed there," and helped the boys along the ridge. Reinhold heard the word "exposed" but did not immediately take in its meaning. On the summit at the iron cross, weathered and pock-marked by lightning, a group of climbers who had just come up the last ridge greeted them. They shook hands, congratulating the two youngsters on their climb. Reinhold felt elated but very tired. It looked a long way down to the meadow bathed in sunshine 3,000 feet below. Up here it was raw and elemental, a narrow platform of rock swept by the wind.

Now they had to go down, reversing those hundreds of holds; looking down directly into the void. He was glad of the rope linking him firmly to his father, glad of the quiet advice given by his mother, glad when they reached the scree, then the shade of the pine trees and at last the soft, springy meadow grass; glad most of all for the warmth of the hay and a comfortable place to sleep. It had been a hard day, even for grown-ups — but especially for a five-year-old.

Villnöss provided a secure childhood for Messner. The valley folk were tough, dependable people but, as Reinhold grew older, they seemed so often dull to him, and unwilling to look beyond the bounds of their small, neat farms.

But the valley itself was never dull, never just a place for farming cattle and crops. It was always far more exciting: a place of changing colour and light rising to a broad upland hollow dotted with buildings and woodland and ending dramatically beneath the walls of the Geisler Alps.

When the war ended the Messner family started to expand, but with thrift. Josef's salary as headmaster covered their needs. There was also a strong post-war compulsion to be as self-sufficient as possible. The steep garden behind the house faced south into the sun and yielded a fine crop of vegetables. Josef became a keen breeder of poultry. The shed at the top of the garden housed a large number of hens which kept the family in eggs and meat and supplemented their income. All the young Messners became expert at caring for poultry.

A wardrobe of hand-me-down clothes passed from one child to the next. When the children required shoes, Maria's grandfather, a tanner, would provide one large piece of leather and a cobbler came to the house for a week to make shoes for the entire family.

It was a close, mutually supportive family life, unsensational but secure, and at holiday time the whole family would hire a pony and trap, stock up with food, bedding and spare clothes and drive up through the forests to the meadow, 3,000 feet above St. Peter.

Thrown in with the supplies went a few hundred feet of hemp rope. Josef took his sons on easy rock climbs in the Geisler Alps. The keenest were Reinhold and Günther who showed a natural ability. Reinhold developed a strong will and as a boy became engrossed in the study of mountains and the men who climbed them. His family's reaction was to look upon his hobby as no more than a channel for his vital nature; a means of letting off steam. Mountain guides worked from Villnöss but climbing was regarded locally in those days as a faintly eccentric pastime for visitors to indulge in.

Josef took his sons on the easy courses above the meadow, always crossing the high pass to the gentler cliffs on the south side and walking beneath the steep walls that rose from the north face of the Geisler peaks.

Reinhold in his early teens had already proved himself a rebel. He deeply enjoyed the security and the life in Villnöss but he was growing to reject some of the simple values of the community. He grew less enchanted by religion, particularly the faith of the Catholics in St. Peter whose lives revolved around the church with its impressive arches, ornamentation and tall bell tower that could send a mellow reminder of God and His requirements into every nook and cranny of the valley. He resented the time spent in church and would sit in the pews, while others prayed, his eyes ranging over the baroque overhangs, cornices and tall plaster pillars, working out moves and climbs. A foothold in that niche there, step up and grab that saint by the nose, straddle between those fretwork bits above the choir stalls, lay back up the organ pipes, or would it be best to hand- and foot-jam between them? Hell of a clatter if the whole lot avalanched!

A quick temper and no gift for holding his tongue led Reinhold into trouble with the parish priest, the mayor of St. Peter and the parents of a schoolmate who plagued him with teasing. Young Messner dealt such punishment to this unfortunate lad that a doctor had to be called to patch him up. Josef was angry and fully in favour of inflicting equal punishment on his son. Maria said no; Reinhold had been basically in the right and had delivered his own justice. That was his privilege. Josef calmed down.

By the late 1950s Reinhold and Günther were taking their younger brothers and sister on walks and climbs in the Geisler Alps. Slowly, a partnership developed between them on easy climbs and then on the grade three routes. When the weather was really fine and the rocks bone dry, Günther would forge a note from their mother and send it to the school, saying they were both ill and unable to go. They would then head for the high meadow on their bicycles, or for one of the outcrops of rock at the foot of the Geisler Alps, and spend the day climbing. They grew exceptionally fit, lithe and powerful. Both were slimly built, but their arms and legs developed a wiry strength. At dusk the brothers would ride home, down the forestry track, bicycle wheels rattling over the rough boulders. Often the track would look like a silver stream reflecting moonlight between the velvet woodland. Everywhere was the sound and scent of mountains: the rich smell of pinewood, the never-ending rush of streams draining the higher ground. Climbing had become a profoundly integral part of both their lives. It was a great exploration and excitement, each climb a fresh insight into themselves and their reactions to fear or enjoyment. In a sense this was the time when the sheer exhilaration of moving over steep ground was most keen, when the challenge was strongest and the boundaries unknown.

In 1959, when he was fourteen, Reinhold went with his father to look at the Castiglioni Route on the Kleine Fermeda — not a spectacular climb, but steep and with a full measure of Dolomite exposure. For Reinhold it was to be a significant expedition. Dolomite cliffs are sensational in that they do not form part of the general angle of a mountain but rise vertically in huge towers. Usually the weather around them is warm, the rock bone dry with high frictional quality and well supplied with holds. In other words, these towers are a joy to climb on.

Josef and Reinhold arrived at the foot of the Castiglioni route and picked out the main features of it. There was a crack that ran up for 20 metres to a ledge, then a series of steep slabs and chimneys ending in a long wall near the summit. Reinhold offered to lead. Josef shrugged his shoulders. He did not wish to accompany Reinhold up the entire route but he was prepared to guard the rope as he led the first pitch. He could then abseil down to the start. He had become very impressed with the way his son moved over rock and the confidence he showed. He quietly hoped that this confidence would not outrun his experience.

Reinhold liked the look of the climb. He clipped the rope into the harness around his waist, arranged a selection of slings and karabiners around his neck and examined the first pitch. The sun shone directly on to the face and the rock felt warm to the touch. When he fingered the first holds he felt the now familiar rush of confidence. He moved upward and with a steady rhythm climbed the pitch, taking in part of the next one as well. The rope between son and father had by this time run out. Reinhold unclipped his end of it and let it fall. His father standing at the foot of the cliff felt the rope become dead, without the steady unwinding pull as the leader progresses.

"Hey, what's happening, Reinhold? The rope is slack," he called up, but his son was already moving on to the third pitch of the climb. Reinhold felt for the first time the delicious commitment of being alone, totally alone on steep exposed rock. No rope could save him if he miscalculated and fell. Each step upwards, each higher hold achieved only added extra certainty to the outcome if he let go. Of course that was not the way to look at it, or so Josef tried to convince himself at the foot of the face.

There was no possibility of letting go. It was not a question of whether or not he would reach the top but of how well he would do the climb. Would that easy rhythm continue? Reinhold became totally absorbed in working out the pattern of holds. He even checked himself from jumping one foot off a toe hold and snatching the other one on to it, a quick technique but one which offends the basic rule of maintaining three points on the rock at all times. Suddenly there was nothing more to climb. The rock ended with the point of the Kleine Fermeda and an unfolding of the familiar view over the high meadow. He had reached the summit quite alone and by a technically difficult route. It was his skill and his judgement that had put him there. In a curious way, the die was cast.

The jagged cliffs of the Geisler Alps became known in every detail to Reinhold and Günther over the next few years. Villnöss often received visiting climbers and the Italian Alpine Club had an active section in the area, but the popularity of the more spectacular mountains in the heart of the Dolomites a few kilometres further south meant that the valley remained a relatively quiet backwater. For the Messner brothers, however, there were no other mountains and in their teens they ticked off more and more of the classic routes. Essentially, the mountains were a part of their lives, whether through rock climbing or walks along the lovely pathways which threaded the hills around the valley; through hunting chamois or, in winter time, ski-towing between the mountain huts.

Unlike some Alpine valleys Villnöss had relatively gently sloping shoulders above the main habitations of St. Peter and St. Magdalena, with large areas of woodland to bind the snow or help defuse the destructive sweep of an avalanche.

Maria herself no longer climbed but she did nothing to discourage the children and Josef kept his own keen interest in his mountains and his hens.

Reinhold and Günther had a minimum of climbing equipment: hardly more than a length of rope and a couple of soft metal pitons. They traversed the faces and climbed cracks and buttresses without having any idea whether or not they had been climbed before; and during all this they were scarcely conscious of the high degree of skill they were attaining. In fact the northern slope of the Geisler peaks demands a high standard of technique because of the large amount of loose rock.

When he was fourteen Reinhold left the village school at St. Peter and went to the High School at Bolzano. But his love for the peaks did not falter. He kept a record of his climbs with Günther at this time, written in thick books packed with postcard pictures of mountains with routes drawn carefully up them, and interspersed with the copied-out work of German poets. Mountaineering was clearly felt to be an exciting and romantic adventure.

Reflecting on those formative years, Reinhold feels they were most important for the way they helped to develop in him an instinct for mountaineering. In any sport a man may reach a certain point through sheer technical ability. Only instinct and a real understanding for his element will take him that subtle step further. Champions in most sports have a "feel" for what they are doing. It was only through constant association with mountains that Messner could draw his own boundaries and set precise limits to what he could attempt. Most of this maturing process was also subconscious: the only conscious objective was the game and the enjoyment.

In his late teens Reinhold decided to become an architect and enrolled at Padua University. His aim was to take an architectural and technical diploma but climbing remained a preoccupation, and every weekend and during the holidays he headed directly for the mountains. He added a number of solo ascents of classic routes in the grade four to five category but he also continued his strong partnership with Günther. His brother was two years younger and still at Bolzano High School but they often met up and climbed together. Reinhold, the dominant big brother, usually set the pace and every outcrop of rock in the broad dull valley north of Bolzano was explored, with longer expeditions when time and money allowed.

Life at university helped to confirm his early intuitions about his home valley. Before he began his course he worked as a teacher at the school in Eppan, a delightful and ancient town north of Bolzano. He enjoyed the work, particularly for the extra resources and the free time it gave him.

By now Reinhold had an ambivalent attachment to the Villnöss valley. It was a wonderful place to come home to but, equally, a wonderful place to leave. His mother, to whom he felt very close, showed great understanding and calmly got on with arranging the practicalities of life for her nine children.

One summer day, Waltraud, the only daughter in this strongly male household, met a stocky cheerful man in St. Peter who said he had come to repair the church spire. His technique was simple but sensational. He would lassoo the top of the tower with a circular collar of rope from which dangled a vertical length. Having ensured that all was firm he would then swarm up the vertical rope and manoeuvre his way to the place which required repair.

The steeplejack's name was Sepp Mayerl and he explained that his work among the dizzier places made by man was extremely helpful as training for his climbs among the natural cathedrals of the Dolomites. ''You must meet my brothers,'' Waltraud said. ''They like climbing, too.''

It was to be a crucially important meeting. Sepp Mayerl was an exceptionally powerful climber, some years older than Reinhold, and very skilled in the art of using pitons and other technical aids which made difficult routes on rock possible. Linking these modern techniques to the natural flair which Reinhold and Günther already possessed was to be an important step in their development as climbers. Sepp Mayerl's calm maturity and tremendous ingenuity taught the brothers a lot about the art of staying alive in unlikely places.

Sepp joined in the Messners' explorations in the Geisler Alps and on other mountains in the Dolomites. Meanwhile, at college in Padua, Reinhold was ploughing through his Gometra training when the first opportunity to earn money from his mountaineering skill occurred. At the end of term Festa della Matricola, one of the contests involved climbing a long pole coated with a thick layer of grease. A huge crowd of people stood at the foot of this greasy pole which shook with the efforts of a crowd of students attempting to form a human pyramid to put their man on top and help him win the 5,000-lira prize. But for years no one had succeeded in reaching the crown at the top — an old bicycle-wheel rim adorned with two plucked chickens, pasta and sausage. However determined and agile, the contestants always slid down the unpleasant pole long before reaching the top, to the jeers and howls of the onlookers.

Messner stood by watching the antics and as he did so he had an idea. A cord tied around the pole at one-third height was still hanging there, so he asked the jury overseeing the attempt whether an aspiring champion would be allowed to use that loop. Yes, replied the judges. The only devices that were forbidden were ladders and nails. Messner therefore immediately entered his name on the list for a solo attempt.

He arrived at the foot of the pole with a small bag from which he took a few pieces of foam rubber which he spread around the base in case the stratagem failed. Then he donned an old camouflage uniform with pockets bulging with fine sand and turned to the pole. He wrapped a length of rope twice round the stem in a prusik loop and gingerly stepped into it. Exactly as he had hoped, it bit through the grease and was held where it was by friction.

Now he reached up and made a second loop, wrapping the dangling end twice around the greasy pole and stepping into it again to gain height.

The crowd became silent as he alternately shuffled the loops higher and higher up the pole, cleaning off the thickest layer of fat and rubbing in sand so that the prusik loops would bite more securely. It was "Technik" — an artificial means of climbing — but a sure way of making progress up an impossible surface. It took him more than two hours, but eventually he reached the top of the pole, pitched the chickens, pasta and sausage into the cheering crowd and slid quickly down to collect his prize.

As the congratulations and drink flowed, Messner thought with a slight smile how easy it was to impress people. By using only common sense and shrewd judgement he had done something of which others were incapable. It was a modest smile but a significant one for the future.

Chapter 4

SET FOR CLIMBING: THE WALKER SPUR

THE COUNTRYSIDE AROUND Padua was flat and featureless and Messner missed having the mountains immediately around him. And the laws of building science that he was drumming into his head were no encouragement for a budding alpinist. At weekends, when the spring sunshine warmed the old rooftops of the city, making the pantiles glow and the blossom on the fruit trees near his college bright with colour, Messner would close his text books and sometimes head for the Rocca Pendice, an outcrop of vertical limestone near the city, and a favourite haunt of climbers who were unable to reach the big mountains but keen to stretch their legs.

It was delectable exercise. The rocks were in places little more than twenty feet high which allowed a climber to push himself beyond the limit and to fall off, on to the grass bank below, without fear of serious injury. Moves which would have been impossibly risky above any greater drop could be rehearsed without danger. The Rocca Pendice was an ideal practice ground and Messner discovered that by availing himself of it he could mingle study with climbing to a standard which kept him in form for the Alps. The moves were identical to the moves on a major pitch. And for testing them seriously under "working conditions", the consequences of falling off the north face of the Rocca Pendice, where the "piccolo" cliff suddenly extended to a face 150 metres high, were the same as falling off a big mountain.

Messner deliberately cultivated the technique of climbing quickly, of moving swiftly and decisively up routes in the fifth grade of difficulty on his practice cliff. He would shoot nimbly up the Via Normal, overtaking a party which was stolidly making its way to the top. Then he would reverse the south face route, run round the foot of the cliff and re-emerge on a second adjoining route well before the party had reached the top of the first. This practice was not one that pleased his fellow climbers who grumbled either that Messner was merely fanning his ego or that he was being a danger to himself and anyone he fell on.

In fact he had a serious aim, which was to develop enough speed and stamina to take him up a 500-metre Dolomite face without resting. Already the ascetic appeal of solo climbing was beginning to influence his attitude towards mountaineering. The purity of overcoming a climbing problem alone and without the jangling ironmongery carried by many climbers was growing ever more attractive.

Each morning before sunlight flooded the lovely old town of Padua, Messner faithfully spent an hour or more running, which he discovered was a sure way to develop endurance. Stamina became almost an obsession with him. He was determined to pack as much strength and staying-power into his lean frame as possible. The hour's run was supplemented by a hanging traverse along a 20 metre length of stout, decorative beading in the students' residence. The other students shook their heads and smiled at this demonic, dangling figure swinging along the wall, fingers and forearms thick with strain. They could not understand what he was doing, but he was clearly determined.

Reinhold had already begun to explore the other climbing world of snow and ice with Günther and Sepp in the mountains 80 kilometres west of Bolzano. The climbs there were totally different from those in the main Dolomites, with long gullies and faces choked with ice. The technique was totally different but he took to it easily under the skilful guidance of Sepp who was one of the most ingenious climbers the Messners had met. He had taught Reinhold and Günther a great deal about the technique of ice climbing and the way to move expeditiously across difficult frozen ground. Within a very few seasons the brothers became equally adept at climbing warm rock, wet rock, vertical ice and the long, exhausting funnels of frozen snow that deadened the fingers and sapped the strength. In the forefront of Reinhold's mind was the certainty that this was an essential step to total proficiency; that the really skilful climber could switch from rock to ice with swift facility, like changing gear crisply in a car. The long, hard routes of the French and Swiss Alps are particularly demanding of this technique.

Once the skills were mastered, climbing, he thought determinedly to himself, was entirely in the mind. The only person you had to convince that a certain route was possible and that you could climb it was yourself. The only ammunition required for this process was a track record long enough and impressive enough to produce a certainty that greater things were possible. There was no more shrewd judge than the man himself when his own life depended on the decision. False courage could not deceive the skilled mountaineer: he knew exactly how afraid, over-stretched or out of his depth he might be. And the time had arrived for Messner to push one step further, to explore beyond the conventional barriers.

By the mid 1960s there were thousands of feet of difficult rock built into his experience, the classic routes that had delighted generations of climbers. Moving over steep ground had become second nature to him. He had seen mountains in a thousand subtle moods and could sense any slight shift in the conditions almost by sniffing the air. Time spent among hills had taught him the significance of a sudden fall in temperature or a change in the wind direction. Certain types of cloud building up high in a clear sky, sending in tendrils from the south-west, were a positive sign of approaching bad weather. Mountains that had been the background and then the centre of his boyhood now dominated his time. He was supremely fit and confident and egoistic enough to try what others had not done. Was this merely for the satisfaction of doing it or for the acclaim it would bring? He would find out.

There had to be a start to his solo ascents, and Messner fixed on the south-west face of the Burél in the Schiara group on the southern fringe of the Dolomites. He had already climbed the route with Konrad Renzler, an Austrian, and could easily recall the moves and difficulties which he calculated it was possible to overcome solo. To jog his memory he slipped into his pocket a sketch of the great "Very Severe" face cut from a magazine, and drove out from Padua.

It was mid-May and the climbing season had hardly started for the higher faces. Messner strolled up to the mountain hut near the Val di Piero and on to the foot of the huge wall that reared steeply above him. He picked out the route, following it up a sound-looking rib that twisted up the face to a band of ochre-coloured rocks. Across the top of these ran a line of overhangs. He checked the straps of his harness and clipped a bunch of pitons to it. He carried a 50-metre length of rope on his back. A torch, anorak and a packet of dried fruit completed his solo outfit.

The first holds felt very steeply set but he moved up them quickly, conserving strength as best he could; not reaching high but keeping his arms low with a powerful circulation of blood in them. The rock felt different from the cliffs of the northern Dolomites, more water-worn and less compact.

One hundred metres of rock drifted by and Messner sensed the shadow of the overhang. The wall plunged away directly beneath the heels of his boots. Only the tips of his limbs were set on holds, his arms holding his body neatly in balance. The line of his climb led to the right of a roof which constituted the crux. The overhang appeared holdless and the route over it was marked by a rusty-looking expansion bolt.

Retreat flashed through his mind but only on the check-list of alternatives. His arms felt strong, there were no tell-tale signs of strain betraying tiredness or a weakening of will. The crux was in the sixth grade, the top of the Alpine register at that time; and beyond the crux there was absolute commitment to an impending wall. Until this point he had made no move which he could not reverse. Once he was launched beyond the overhang there would be no way but upwards.

Messner had devised a rope system for solo climbing which provided some degree of protection. As he climbed he would run the rope through karabiners clipped into pitons with the "dead" end of the rope running back to a prusik knot at his waist, thus forming a protective circle of rope into which he was tied.

As he progressed he could extend the circle as necessary and at a safe belay could unfasten the prusik and pull the full length of rope free. How well the system would have worked in the event of a fall was hard to calculate and Messner was determined not to find out. He had never fallen off whilst leading a climb but now, surely, on a grade six climb at the greatest point of difficulty he must be near the limits of adhesion to the rock. He tried to recollect how hard this route had been the first time but could only remember the vague blur of movements over the hard section. There was a big difference between being on this wall with a companion and being here like a solitary fly with no one to share the risk, the decisions or the lead.

Messner massaged his arms, pressing blood into the tense, strong muscles at his wrists. He curled and uncurled his fingers and, having made himself as secure as possible with the circle of rope, launched himself out beyond the ring bolt. It was a cool day and the cliff was partly shadowed. The face was out of the wind but as he pulled firmly round the overhang on to the final steeply-pitched wall he looked up and saw clouds racing across the clifftop and strands of grass drifting slowly down through space. His whole body was now arched against the rock. Carefully selecting his holds, he moved at optimum speed, not so fast that he spoiled his calculated rhythm yet not so slowly that the strength in his arms and fingers, already stretched by the pull round the lip of the overhang, would give out either through nervous strain from being so alone or through sheer exhaustion.

The angle slackened. The change was almost imperceptible but he felt the impact of it so strongly after so much vertical stress, that it seemed as if the cliff had flattened out. There was no longer such a fearsome drag of gravity on every point and Messner had the sensation of stepping on to a ladder. Swiftly he soared up the final few metres to the top where he sat down panting for breath, more from excitement than tiredness.

Another boundary had been broken, another piece set in the jigsaw of what he would personally be able to achieve. Good; what next?

As he matured through college, Messner developed a mercurial and decisive nature. He was a conscientious but not brilliant student and it was obvious to him when he entered Padua University in 1967 that mountaineering would always have first importance in his life — above designing houses. But who could earn a living from climbing mountains? He could become a guide, of course, but he wanted far more from climbing than escorting clients up undemanding routes. His mountaineering was powerful and commanding. It was already clear that his talent for climbing was extraordinary, but none of his contemporaries was able to exist on this talent alone and all his heroes, including the great Herman Bühl, had either endured pinchpenny lives or been backed by private means.

Gaston Rébuffat, the French guide, in a sense pointed the way with his series of books and films. It was clear that to live off mountains you had to grasp public attention by constantly moving one step ahead of convention, by either shocking or stunning the world into wanting to read about your exploits.

These questing thoughts entered Messner's mind at university but were not the force that drove him on to attempt more and more extraordinary climbs. At this time the seven great north faces of the Alps were the target for aspiring "tigers" in the climbing world but the guide books to the Alps contained innumerable routes on many hundreds of cliffs, each route graded and dissected into pitches. The challenge was to develop individual skill to a degree where any existing route could be repeated and where mountain instinct and an eye for a new line could take the climber on to untried ground. The other recognised way to a new dimension in climbing was to complete routes in better time or with less protection than had previously been possible.

Both these distinctions appealed to Messner who had grown to dislike the artificial nature of Alpine rock climbing. The easy routes in the Alps which he had climbed when he was a boy were festooned with ladders and strung with fixed ropes at every exposed place. They were a scarring but necessary fixture on the trade routes, allowing a maximum number of undertrained but eager amateurs to reach a summit and admire the view. But the passion for riveted security had begun to spread far beyond the easier routes, out on to the open rock faces themselves. Routes were being raped at pistol point, or rather bolt-gun or chisel point. Climbers, so the arguments of the purists went, were carrying their courage in their rucksacks. If there were no holds to move to on a particular face, no cracks into which the slimmest piton would sink, then out came the bolt gun and bang! a hole instantly appeared into which an expansion bolt capable of holding several tons could easily be fitted.

By this time, in the late sixties, Messner had a long and rapidly growing list of classic routes, hard routes, new routes and solo ascents in his curriculum vitae. His reputation among the best alpinists was established and his dogmatic nature made him unshy about making his views public. When he was eighteen and at High School in Bolzano his keenness on climbing had caught the attention of the editor of the local newspaper, the *Dolomitten*, who asked him to write a series of articles about the subject.

One of these articles, entitled "The Murder of the Impossible", written when in his early twenties described such methods of attacking a mountain as unsporting. Years later he would not seek to improve the strength or directness of the sentiments.

"What have I personally got against 'direttissimas'?" he wrote. "Nothing at all; in fact, I think that the 'falling drop of water' route is one of the most logical things that exist. And of course it always has existed — so long as the mountain permits it. But sometimes the line of weakness wanders to the left or the right of this line; and then we see climbers — those on the first ascent, I mean — going straight on up as if it weren't so, striking in bolts of course. Why do they go that way? 'For the sake of freedom,' they say; but they don't realise that they are slaves of the plumbline.

"They have a horror of deviations. 'In the face of difficulties, logic commands one not to avoid them, but to overcome them,' declares Paul Claudel. And that's what the direttissima protagonists say, too, knowing from the start that the equipment they have will get them over any obstacle. They are therefore talking about problems which no longer exist. Could the mountain stop them with unexpected difficulties? They smile: those times are long past! The impossible in mountaineering has been eliminated, murdered by the direttissima.

"Yet direttissimas would not in themselves be so bad were it not for the fact that the spirit that guides them has infiltrated the entire field of climbing. Take a climber on a rock face, iron rungs beneath his feet and all around him only yellow, overhanging rock. Already tired, he bores another hole above the last peg. He won't give up. Stubbornly, bolt by bolt, he goes on. *His* way, and none other, must be forced on the face.

"Expansion bolts are taken for granted nowadays; they are kept to hand just in case some difficulty cannot be overcome by ordinary methods. Today's climber doesn't want to cut himself off from the possibility of retreat. Rock faces are no longer overcome by climbing skill, but are humbled, pitch by pitch, by methodical manual labour; what isn't done today will be done tomorrow. Free-climbing routes are dangerous, so they are protected by pegs. Ambitions are no longer built on skill, but on equipment and the length of time available. The decisive factor isn't courage, but technique; an ascent may take days and days, and the pegs and bolts be counted in hundreds. Retreat has become dishonourable, because everyone knows now that a combination of bolts and single-mindedness will get you up anything, even the most repulsive-looking direttissima.

"Times change, and with them concepts and values. Faith in equipment has replaced faith in oneself; a team is admired for the number of bivouacs it makes, while the courage of those who still climb 'free' is derided as a manifestation of lack of conscientiousness.

"Who has polluted the pure spring of mountaineering?

"The innovators perhaps wanted only to get closer to the limits of possibility. Today, however, every single limit has vanished, been erased. In principle, it didn't seem to be a serious matter, but ten years have sufficed to eliminate the word 'impossible' from mountaineering vocabulary.

"Progress? Today, ten years from the start of it all, there are a lot of people who don't care where they put bolts, whether on new routes or on classic ones. People are drilling more and more and climbing less and less.

" 'Impossible': it doesn't exist any more. The dragon is dead, poisoned, and the hero Siegfried is unemployed. Now anyone can work on a rock face, using tools to bend it to his own idea of possibility.

"Some people foresaw this a while ago, but they went on drilling, both on direttissimas and on other climbs, until they lost the taste for climbing: why dare, why gamble, when you can proceed in perfect safety? And so they became the prophets of the direttissima: 'Don't waste time on classic routes — learn to drill, learn to use your equipment. Be cunning: if you want to be successful use every means you can to get round the mountain. The era of the direttissima has barely begun; every peak awaits its plumbline route. There's no rush, for a mountain can't run away — and nor can it defend itself.'

" 'Done the direttissima yet? And the super direttissima?' These are the criteria by which mountaineering prowess is measured nowadays. And so the young men go off, crawl up the ladder of bolts, and then ask the next ones: 'Done the direttissima yet?'

"Anyone who doesn't play ball is laughed at for daring to take a stand against current opinion. The plumbline generation has already consolidated itself and has thoughtlessly killed the ideal of the impossible. Anyone who doesn't oppose this makes himself an accomplice of the murderers. When future mountaineers open their eyes and realise what has happened, it will be too late: the impossible (and, with it, risk) will be buried, rotted away, and forgotten forever.

"All is not yet lost, however, although 'they' are returning to the attack; and even if it's not always the same people, it'll be other people similar to them. Long before they attack, they'll make a great noise, and once again any warning will be useless. They'll be ambitious and they'll have long holidays — and some new 'last great problem' will be resolved. They'll leave more photographs at the hut, as historical documents, showing a dead straight line of dots running from base to summit — and on the face itself, several hundred bolts. Newspapers, radio and television will once again inform us that 'man has achieved the impossible.'

"If people have already been driven to the idea of establishing a set of rules of conduct, it means that the position is serious; but we young people don't want a mountaineering code. On the contrary, 'up there we want to find long, hard days, days when we don't know in the morning what the evening will bring.' But for how much longer will we be able to have this?

"I'm worried about that dead dragon: we should do something before the impossible is finally interred. We have hurled ourselves, in a fury of pegs and bolts, on increasingly savage rock faces: the next generation will have to know how to free itself from all these unnecessary trappings. We have learned from the plumbline routes; our successors will once again have to reach the summits by *other* routes.

"It's time we repaid our debts and searched again for the *limits of possibility* — for we must have such limits if we are going to use the virtue of courage to approach them. And we must never break them down again, even if it's impossible for us to reach them. Where else will we be able to find refuge in our flight from the oppression of everyday humdrum routine? In the Himalaya? In the Andes? Yes, certainly, if we can get there; but for most of us there'll only be these old Alps.

"So let's save the dragon; and in the future let's follow the road that past climbers marked out. I'm convinced it's still the right one.

"Put on your boots and get going. If you've got a companion, take a rope with you and a couple of pitons for your belays, but nothing else. I'm already on my way, ready for anything — even for retreat, if I meet the impossible. I'm not going to be killing any dragons, but if anyone wants to come with me, we'll go to the top together on the routes we can climb without branding ourselves as murderers." English translation from *Mountain* No. 15, 1971.

There were periods when Reinhold's free time at Padua became a bewildering swirl of climbs; his list of summits and cliffs lengthened, as did the number of new routes or second ascents that he completed. Messner's other climbing partners at this time were Sepp Mayerl, the steeplejack; Heinl Messner, another powerful climber from Villnöss (no relation — Messner is a common name); and Heindl Holzer, a young firebrand from Merano. Holzer was a short, immensely powerful man who made up for his lack of height with an overwhelming Napoleonic manner. Not only did Heindl seek to climb the most difficult routes; he became renowned for his skill at skiing down sheer faces. Alas, one sheer descent proved too many when in 1977 he fell and was killed.

The Messner brothers were now full of confidence and determined to experience the world well beyond Villnöss, so with the help of their father's motorcycle they explored mountain areas in the far reaches of the Dolomites. Their first foray into the Western Alps in 1965 was a tentative venture, however; they attempted the Bonatti route on the Matterhorn but retreated because of bad weather and then climbed the Courtes north face. Even for this they were still dogged by the appalling weather and found themselves heading upwards into snow and mist as everyone else was heading back to the hut. A brief glimpse of the 1,000-metre face of the Grandes Jorasses, glinting blackly across the Vallée Blanche, confirmed in Reinhold an ambition to climb this jutting rib that rose out of its frozen sea like the bows of some monster ship. He had studied photographs of the ridge and already had its main features filed away in his memory, but the actual sight of that gaunt prow rising from the folds of the Léschaux Glacier was a dramatic jolt. It would be a superb climb because, being steeply inclined, it was not continually swept by avalanches like so many of the other great north faces. The objective dangers would be relatively few and the focus would be on mountaineering skill. And they would be following in the holds of Ricardo Cassin who had led the first successful ascent, and Walter Bonatti who had accounted for the first winter ascent.

It was the following summer (1966) that Reinhold returned to Chamonix. The season had started poorly but a spell of fine weather coincided with his arrival along with Sepp Mayerl, Peter Habeler and Fritz Zambra from the East Tyrol.

Standing in the warm sun, the climbers looked at the impressive cirque of mountains from the café at Montenvers. A blinding light was reflected by the Mer de Glace and through the powerful telescope they could minutely examine the rock faces of the peaks around them. Their gaze was naturally drawn to the gothic spire of the Aiguille du Dru, standing up from the Aiguille Verte, but Reinhold was delighted to see that Peter kept swinging the big lens back in the direction of the Walker Spur on the Grandes Jorasses. Sepp was doubtful. The guides in Chamonix had turned their mouths down at the mention of the route. There was far too much fresh snow about, they said. The Walker Spur was too high, too exposed and would be sheathed in ice from bottom to top. The younger members of the party were not impressed by this gloom. Fresh snow had indeed settled on the Grandes Jorasses but this would be less of a danger on the Walker Spur. The weather forecast in Chamonix was promising with a breast of high pressure settled like a hen on its nest above the town. Sepp, the senior climber in the party, was persuaded by the enthusiasm of the others and they set out for the Léschaux Hut, determined to make an attempt on the face the following day.

At 3 a.m. in the darkness of the small wooden shelter, they were woken by the early call of the wind, banging against the door frame. Sepp lit the lamp which cast a cold light over the three figures muffled in their sleeping bags like reclining modern sculptures. Reluctantly they rose. There was the thud of heavy boots on the plank floor, the clink of tempered ironmongery and the heavy rustle of gaiters being pulled on. Breath clouded in the freezing air. It was always a dull, numbing feeling waking up on the morning of a climb. Muscles rebelled at the early exercise, as sluggish as the freezing darkness outside, and there was tension in the pit of the stomach at the prospect of a sixth grade climb.

The rocks of the Walker Spur soared immediately above the bank of the glacier and the four of them tracked down to the start by torchlight. It was difficult because the edge of the glacier between the hut and the start of the rocks was heavily crevassed and broken. At the first cold filtering of dawn the immense black pillar emerged from the night above them. The snow surface where the Jorasses reared up from the glacier was perfectly firm. Even so they roped up; Messner to Zambra in front, Mayerl to Habeler following close behind.

They moved swiftly until the way was blocked by a rock step sheathed in ice. Messner struck the smooth surface with the blade of his axe and it rang with a dangerously hollow sound. The guides had been correct, but surely they could climb the ice, front-pointing on crampons delicately up the glazed slabs? They continued, the hard surface tilting up now at a steeper angle. This was the easy section; how could they contemplate the extreme pitches higher up? Below the Rébuffat crack, Messner made half a dozen tries at the ice-choked pitch leading to the safe ledge. He felt exhausted and allowed Peter and Sepp to take over the lead. Now that they had decided to make the attempt, Sepp was in great humour, his solid, muscular figure moving relentlessly over the difficult ground. Messner was even more impressed by the performance of Peter Habeler, whose style was neat, perfectly confident and amazingly swift.

Conditions were wintry. The two ropes inched up the Rébuffat crack, across the exposed traverse and up towards the Cassin bivouac. The day had slipped by and already the peaks about Montenvers were casting long, dark shadows over the glacier. They would certainly not make the summit that day.

The first third of the face ended at an open corner some 80 metres high which was filled solidly with ice, so that the pitons that were in place were buried. Bridging the ice, Sepp Mayerl moved steadily up the pitch. On this section it was not possible to hurry; safety depended on the leader moving with absolute care.

It was dark by the time the four climbers had belayed themselves on to the two steep ledges of the Cassin bivouac. They were muffled up for warmth, bivouac sacks pulled up around their legs, but the cold crept in just the same, prodding them out of their half-sleep with juddering callousness.

Messner later wrote in his diary: "This then was the Walker Spur, and this was me sitting here, freezing cold and with my toes gone to sleep. No way off now, but we should have enough pegs and ice screws to get us to the top.

"The feeling spread in me that for the time being we were safe because, like it or not, there was nothing we could do here in the bivouac at night; it was a comforting thought but at the same time disturbing. My whole body craved warmth and rest. But the continuing night was like a blanket

on which I sat. I did not sleep, or shut my eyes any more; tiredness
weighed like lead in my arms and legs. I had the uneasy feeling that I
could no longer think what I wanted to think. I had no power over my
thoughts. They wandered at will and always harked back to the unnerving
prospect of steep, glazed slabs, chimneys packed with compressed snow
and vertical spurs.''

It was an unpleasant, half-conscious limbo in which the mind became
transfixed with fears that would be briskly swept aside if one were fully
awake. Slowly the sky filled with pale colour, then the sun began to
animate the tips of the Aiguilles with stinging lashes of light. The four
climbers struggled out of their bivouac sacks, banged circulation and
warmth into frozen feet and hands and set the small stove going. But it
was not until the first pitch of the day was behind him that any real
warmth or fluency spread through Messner. The bivouac ledge had been
sheltered from the full strength of the wind that had blown during the
night and cleared the fresh snow from the rocks. They climbed faster now
up the long granite ridge, noting the famous features along the route,
constantly alert in case they lost the complicated line and wasted more
time. The climbing surface was in appalling condition further up and
constantly they had to strap and unstrap their crampons with numbed,
irritated fingers as bare rock was followed by ice and then reverted to
pitches of cold, raw granite unmarked by the previous passage of others.
The difficult conditions compounded the sense of triumph, however,
when in the late afternoon the four climbers stood on the Pointe Walker
of the Grandes Jorasses.

Chapter 5

A SEASON OF PLENTY

BY 1969 REINHOLD MESSNER had built a formidable reputation as an "extreme" mountaineer. If there was any doubt about his leading position in a sport where competition was understated yet intense, his mastery was confirmed in the summer of that year with a phenomenal spate of extremely difficult Alpine routes. He was in top form physically.

The climbs over the previous two summers and winters had given him a profound understanding of mountains which provided him with an immediate grasp of route, line, condition. He completed his studies at Padua and received his Gometra diploma in the spring of 1969, but climbing was by now a total preoccupation. It overwhelmed any other interest, dominated his friendships and commanded all his spare time. He believed his climbing record so far was a strong enough bedrock on which to build more new achievements.

Günther remained a close climbing partner, too, and it was at this time that Peter Habeler, who was another of Sepp Mayerl's climbing companions, stepped into the circle.

But in mountaineering there is always a background noise of danger. It is persistently there, rumbling in an avalanche or rolling in the thunder of an approaching storm. Sometimes it is loud and awesome, as when lightning bombards the rocks, making metal glow and hair stand on end. At other times it may be the sudden fracture of a rock, weakened by a winter of ice and giving way beneath an unsuspecting hand.

The most unnerving type of fear infects a climber when he believes that he is going to have to let go. Usually a rock climber will avoid being thrust into this ultimate hazard by carefully obeying the ground rules, but in every climbing life mistakes are sometimes made. For Messner, whose fingers and toes had by that time taken him safely up many sheer kilometres of rock face, the *mauvais pas* occurred on the central pillar of the Heiligkreuzkofel. It was not in a part of the Dolomites which was noted for the challenging quality of its routes. The Livanos Pfeiler was the best

57

known route here and Reinhold and Günther climbed it in the summer of 1969, taking two days and converting many of the artificial pitches into free climbs. Günther had spent several days preparing and examining the route up the impressive 600-metre pillar, but it was not until the two brothers were scaling it that Reinhold noticed a second, less marked pillar towards the centre of the face.

This intrigued them, so they returned to the crag after completing the first route and set about the unclimbed central pillar. It was a dry day, the rock was warm and as Reinhold climbed he did not feel in any sense out of form. There was no hesitation in his moves from hold to hold, no tension in the muscles that lifted him fluently up the rock. The rope snaked out, pitch after pitch, until the drop beneath their boots was 500 metres and the angle showed no sign of relenting.

Then they came to it. A broad ledge running across the pillar and above it a totally blank wall. Reinhold balanced on the ledge and scanned the wall. Nothing. Glancing down between his feet he could see Günther's helmet as his brother stood on the belay some 20 metres below, releasing the rope to him as Reinhold moved. There was no way of avoiding the pitch without making a very artificial kink in an otherwise smooth line. Yet there were no cracks to make a natural home for a piton, only a very smooth slab of dolerite with indifferent friction. Reinhold reached up the wall and found two small indents. Then he moved. His body obeyed the summons and curved out in a delicate arch, tensed on the tiny holds. He had gained another metre, but the tension was stiffening his arms and the muscles in his calves began to ache. Still no actual doubt crossed his mind. This was thin, extremely thin even by the usual micrometer-screw standards that relate the steepness of the face to the size and shape of the holds. If Mr Micawber had been a rock climber, two millimetres of boot tip on a two millimetre hold would have meant happiness; no boot tip on anything, infinite sadness.

He made another move and felt, for the first time, a tingle of doubt. He knew that soon the hot pain of cramp would come to muscles that would have to keep on working flat out however convulsed they were. He could control that. But more than the pain he would have to control the fear, that sensation which could make even a safe toehold seem an insecure support. The right hand moved up again. Fingers stiff with stress found nothing. And again the body arched, like a longbow at full strain.

Günther could feel the tension transmitted down the rope. He had looked up when Reinhold's smooth upward progress had halted; now he could see his brother poised on the slab, a wide space between his body and the rock, perfectly controlled but on nothing. He quickly calculated the distance of the fall; at least fifteen metres, then another fifteen before the rope jarred, by which time Reinhold would be reaching almost unstoppable velocity. At least it would be a clear fall; the cliff was so sheer.

His entire body quivering with the strain of holding on, Reinhold mentally checked his options. It would be impossible to reverse the last four or five moves. He could recollect them perfectly but the different pattern of movement downward would be too much for the laws of adhesion. If he fell in the process, it could turn into an awkward plunge too close to the rock. Better to fall well clear of the face until the rope could brake you — or break itself.

He had remained motionless for almost a minute. The predicament was excruciating and a fine smear of sweat was forming on the tips of his fingers. He decided that he must make one more move upwards to project himself in an arc away from the rock and into space: one more move to allow the inexorable force of gravity to take over, to cartwheel him through a thousand feet of emptiness.

His body straightened with one smooth dynamic upward thrust. Every muscle was screaming as the tips of his Vibram soles gave a parting kiss to the slab and yet, incredibly to him, he remained tentatively pinned on the rock face. The right fingers landed again a few centimetres higher and the skin moulded itself into a roughness in the rock as tenuous as braille print. There was nothing to claw, nothing for the finger joints to hook on to but just enough to keep the hands from slithering. Messner's mind reeled. He had prepared himself for falling off and yet he was still here. His left hand reached higher up the slab, finger tips angled over a minute flaw in the rock, which felt as big as a parallel bar. Adrenalin and hope surged through his body. Bend that damned arm. Arch the body. The right fingers have joined the left. A few more centimetres. Pull. His boot tips grazed the slab, clawing for adhesion. The left arm lashed out again and mercifully struck a positive edge along the top of the slab. The last ebb of power brought him gasping on to a narrow ledge, which might have been as wide as the Sahara.

Messner struggled to control his breathing, to stop his heart pounding. There was no fear now, only a great exhilaration at having leapt through a fire of awareness. He pulled in the rope tightly. The fluent partnership — with his brother and with life — was back in action.

After his experience on the Heiligkreuzkofel fear rarely entered his system. His climbing had become almost a reflex, a relentless force compounded by a great affection for the Alps. He wanted to devote his life to mountaineering if that were possible, but the only way to achieve that ideal state of existence was by doing something that no one else had done. He determined to stay one step ahead of the game, but always to keep the risk to the minimum.

When Messner left university with a qualification and a profession at which to earn a living, his father's sigh of relief was audible from Villnöss to Padua. But Josef was quickly robbed of any ideas that his son would settle down in Villnöss and lead an ordinary life. A telegram from Otti Wiedmann of the Austrian Alpine Club in Innsbruck arrived in the middle of May offering his self-willed offspring a place on the club's expedition to Peru and Messner accepted immediately.

Reinhold had never before been outside Europe but within three days he had got together all the visas, suffered a variety of vaccinations and on May 25 was on board the plane to Rio de Janeiro. It was Messner's first expedition and with him went Peter Habeler who had also been invited at the last minute to represent the committee of the premier Austrian Club. The weather was stubbornly Alpine — cold, grey and wet — and when they reached the area of Yerupaja Grande, the target for the expedition, they heard that the east face of the mountain had fallen to an American team the previous summer.

Little was known about the detail of the route taken, but talks with local porters and Indians who had observed the climb made it clear that the Americans had kept well towards the right-hand side of the face. The direct route still remained. Quite like the Alps, Messner thought wryly. Even in this remote corner of the world climbers were beavering away to snatch the best line, to be first to a new inaccessible point.

On June 3 the nine climbers of the Tyrolean Andes Expedition departed into the Cordillera Huayhuash. Among them were Peter Habeler and Sepp Mayerl, Messner's climbing mentor. They travelled at first in a rented bus. Then came a three day march, following in the wake of 28 mules and three horses through steep-sided gorges and across picturesque plateaux to the foot of the mountain. The base camp was at 4,150 metres and the summit 6,634. Almost 2,500 metres of climbing, no more than some of the major Alpine routes Messner had completed. But how would the extra altitude affect him? Habeler was asking himself the same question.

The mountain remained firmly covered in cloud, hiding its wild appearance, but the climbers went about the patient business of setting up a series of camps and by June 13 had reached 5,300 metres with a substantial line of fixed ropes to ensure rapid reinforcements of equipment and food should they become necessary.

Rarely could they see the mountain they were attempting to climb. Drenching cloud and squalls of sleet whipped across the face but occasionally from base camp the full bulk of Yerupaja came into view, a towering mass of steep ice and rock with a tall south-east pillar on the left and two ice fields divided by a broad cliff.

Everyone worked at lifting loads of stores to the two higher camps. Another 450 metres of fixed rope were laced to the south-east pillar leading to a third camp at 5,750 metres.

On June 14 Peter and Reinhold launched the first attack on the east face. They had shown already that they were exceptionally fit and able to move at high speed together. They left Camp I at 3 a.m. and crossed bands of steep rock below Camp II into a deep hollow on the east wall. Their altimeter read 5,280 metres. There remained over 1,300 metres of ice above them, rising at an average angle of about 60 degrees. At 6 a.m., in the grey light, they moved on to the face itself. As they climbed the sun came out, the first strong sunshine they had seen during the entire expedition. It was no blessing because the warmth loosened stones frozen into the ice so that a lethal barrage fell constantly around them. They had covered 200 metres before they agreed to retreat and try again when the stones were frozen into the face.

On June 17 the two climbers set up a camp in the hollow and at 2 a.m. the next day set out once again with minimum loads for the greatest speed. Both accepted that they would have to avoid a bivouac at all costs. With this thought to spur them on they moved rapidly up the ice wall and by the time the sun was directly on the face were level with the crest of the south-east pillar. The worst problems of the face lay below them.

The ridge above the pillar was blocked by the vertical rickety mass of rocks which form the summit. They tried to climb it but with the altimeter reading 22 metres short of the true top, gingerly retreated. The risk was too great. At 3 p.m. after a rest they began the descent via the east wall, moving at incredible speed. Less than four hours later they were safe in the camp in the hollow cooking a meal.

On the south-east pillar, the Tyroleans had been busy above Camp III. Sepp Mayerl distinguished himself as a true steeplejack, fixing length upon length of rope so that by June 21 a secure line 1,050 metres long stretched up the rock face. The next day Sepp and Egon Wurm from Innsbruck found the summit ridge to be extremely steep and dangerous. They were forced to bivouac at 6,500 metres, below the summit rocks that had defeated Reinhold and Peter. The following day they too abandoned a direct assault, traversing to the right and then doubling back along the opposite ridge. At 2 p.m. they were on the summit. They descended the east face but were forced to spend a second night and then brave the morning fusillade of stones. At 9 a.m. the expedition could relax. They were all safe in the east face camp.

The expedition was a significant one for Messner. It made him confident that he could command the same remarkable speed and assurance on high mountains that he had developed in the Alps and that high altitude need not be a serious handicap; indeed he found that climbing in thin air had a powerful effect on his stamina. He felt in finest form and determined to make a real assault on those domestic Alpine frontiers when he got back. He had taken a cross-country run from base camp every day, even when he was supposed to be resting, and deliberately ran on his toes so that the exercise would strengthen his calves. By the time he returned from Peru in early spring he had lost more than two stones in weight. His reappearance in Italy caused relief and consternation to his friends and family, for unbeknown to him a newspaper had reported that he had perished in Peru. Messner was able to respond with a wry grin that reports of his death had been greatly exaggerated.

Far from being dead he was about to start his most remarkable Alpine season. His first serious sixth grade solo had been two years before, on the Solda route of the Piz Ciavazes. Since then he had grown to enjoy climbing alone on a great Alpine face. His exploits had begun to make him famous but he had many critics, particularly people who thought he was mad or seeking danger for danger's sake. It was not so, but they were entitled to their view.

For someone who aimed at such dangerous heights it might seem that he led a charmed existence, yet not only he, but none of his friends had been badly injured or died in mountaineering accidents. Death was something that did not stalk climbers inside his own small circle. It happened in the early days of climbing or to people who attempted climbs for which they did not have the experience, but Messner and his friends were skilled enough to have a built-in margin of error. Luck helped too, but luck was regarded as a sanctuary for fools. A climber should be able to endure bad luck and still survive.

With Günther, Reinhold had climbed over 1,000 Alpine routes, more than 40 of them in the highest grades of difficulty. Of course there was a certain amount of unavoidable risk and the more he climbed at this high standard, the more likely was he to be killed. But the delicious paradox was that the more he climbed the greater his assurance and skill would become and the less likely was he to have an accident.

Logically there seemed to be additional risks in climbing on his own, but with such assurance in some senses he was better off alone. He knew precisely his own moods and abilities; even with Günther and Peter he could not know his partner so well. The critics were fierce, but always there was that lean, confident figure with the thatch of dark hair, the huge rucksack and the slightly impudent grin to confound them.

The central pillar of Frêney on the east face of Mont Blanc ranks among Europe's most serious routes; 700 metres of steeply-pitched granite set above the shattered upper basin of the Frêney glacier. Even the route to the foot of the climb is a serious expedition. In 1961 the cream of climbers from France and Italy attempted to solve what then was the greatest problem in the Alps after attempts by each country individually had failed in the previous two years. On July 8 1961 at the bivouac box on the Col de la Fourche, the French climbers Mazeaud, Kohlman, Guillaume and Vieille were settling down for the night before making a third attempt the next day, when the Italians Bonatti, Oggione and Gallieni suddenly arrived with the same plan in mind. The following day the weather was bad but on July 10 all the climbers set out and spent the next four days in freezing cold and bitter winds before deciding to retreat. They made a long succession of abseils down the face and on to the glacier where, exhausted, they bivouacked in a crevasse on the Col de Peuterey. Next day, through cold, exhaustion and exposure, four of them died. It was a month later that the Frêney Pillar was eventually climbed by a team including the British climbers Chris Bonington, Ian Clough and Don Whillans.

Now, in June 1969 eight years later, Messner arrived in Chamonix where he found Erich Lackner, an Austrian climber, waiting for him. Lackner was a big man with enormously powerful arms developed through boxing — not the sort of figure well adapted to delicate rock climbing, but his record of severe routes in the Alps was impressive. Messner had just climbed the North Face of Les Droites but since conditions were promising the two men set off directly for the La Fourche bivouac hut.

Before dawn the next day the two men left the hut and headed towards the huge cliff which was behind, but actually invisible from, the bivouac. The ground was extremely complex and they mistook the lamps of climbers above them, on their way to the Brenva face, for stars. The steep couloir leading to the Col de Peuterey was a deadly maze of crevasses and so they paused to wait for first light. The dawn brought a superb day. As the morning sun strengthened and they approached the foot of the huge pillar, the air grew warm, though a faint breeze stirring across the glacier kept the temperature pleasant. The face started to melt down to the bare rock, and water trickling from verglas splashed down the slabs and gullies. The rock surface began to shimmer with reflected heat. After a while, drifting down from the huge, apparently empty face above them, they heard a cry of someone urgently demanding a rope. Then in the intricate pattern of cracks and bulges they caught sight of a small figure pinned beneath an overhang which was one of the key pitches on the climb.

"Is he all right?" Messner demanded.

"Hard to tell from here. He looks very still and seems to be dangling on the rope."

"We'll get closer."

The figure suddenly thrashed around in a great effort and climbed back up the rope to the roof. He stretched out his legs and arms and pulled himself on to a stance above the overhang. Messner later learned that he had spent over an hour on the pitch.

Messner and Lackner were climbing swiftly up the warm rock, enjoying the splendid situation of the Frêney Pillar and marvelling at their good luck in having such a day for the climb. The sun's warmth was loosening bigger pieces of ice higher up the face which rattled down the wall. It was fine work along the very edge of the buttress and the two climbers led through pitch after pitch to a point where Messner, lured to his right by a piton, suddenly found himself in the centre of an extremely steep wall thinly served with holds. It required a simian move to a small knob of rock projecting up to the right before a long pull brought less steep rock within reach.

At the belay he took in the rope and Lackner plodded straight up the main edge of the buttress, by-passing Messner's extreme manoeuvres on the left.

The two climbers ahead, so it transpired, were Bulgarians on the Chamonix meet of the École Nationale du Ski d'Alpinisme. They had struggled over the main difficulties and their relief showed as they headed up easier rocks to the summit. They had started on their climb at the same time as Messner was beginning his climb of Les Droites.

Lackner reached the foot of the huge plinth of granite called the Candle and began a determined lay-back up a detached flake to the left edge. Hand over hand he ascended until his progress was stopped by a jutting roof. He belayed and took in the rope as Messner drifted up the crack, revelling in the warm, rough touch of the granite.

Lackner rested on the stance, his big body secured by an assortment of ropes clipped to pitons under the roof. Then Messner swung directly past him along the crack and belayed in an étrier at the full scope of the rope. Lackner without a word followed up the crack to the roof, scowled at the impending crack and launched himself at it, jamming in his huge boxer's arms and swinging himself free, his legs dangling in space. Only his grunts and hissing breath disturbed the silence, plus the occasional dislodged rock which suddenly accelerated away towards the foot of the pillar, exploding in splinters and a puff of smoke as it ricocheted to a halt.

Beneath Messner's feet spread the grey creases of the glacier which lay like an enormous dissected brain in the shrivelling summer heat. Beyond the glacier was a solidified ocean of pine forests, and over the valley where Chamonix lay was a tangible film of haze.

The rest of the day drifted by in a delectable series of pitches and they reached the summit just as the setting sun threw the shadow of Mont Blanc eastwards in a gigantic cone. The air remained still and absolutely quiet and in bright moonlight the two climbers descended the mountain, reaching the Col de la Fourche within twelve hours of leaving it — a record for the climb.

At the hut they met the Bulgarians who were celebrating their own success and planning to return to Chamonix the following day. Messner and his partner decided they were in such fine form they might as well keep on climbing for as long as the weather held. The next day they made their target the Pilier Bergland on Les Droites, an unclimbed stretch of extremely steep rock which grew out of a rather hidden corner of the Argentière Basin.

They cut down their weight of gear to the absolute minimum, repacking their rucksacks several times and including only what was essential for survival since they expected the route would be demanding and intricate. They were right. From the start the Pilier Bergland was challenging: Messner stepped on to the rocks above the bergschrund and banged home a knife-blade piton. Suspended from it he swung to the left and worked his way up delicate holds, calling to Lackner to watch the rope carefully; he might be rejoining him any second! A slab of smooth, slippery rock was overcome by balance and uncertain friction. Cracks choked with ice followed, then broken rock; and then a series of grooves which led to the top of a tower halfway up the face. At this point there was an obvious ledge which Lackner had pointed to as a possible bivouac site.

They carried on past it, leading alternately up a succession of cracks and grooves which, however appalling they looked from below, remained just within the bounds of possibility. Finally, a number of rock pinnacles led to the top.

A fine, difficult route it had been; one for the book, Erich agreed. So in good spirits the pair quickly descended the south face of the mountain unroped. As they neared the edge of the glacier, Messner pointed rightwards and they traversed above the crevasse formed by the bergschrund. He was looking for a point from which to gain the glacier when a rushing sound made him look round. Lackner had started off a small slide of snow on the heat-logged slope.

The first trickle of heavy, granulated clumps quickly became a solid carpet of snow avalanching towards the point, 50 metres below, where Messner was standing directly above the crevasse. He rammed his ice axe into the surface and clung to it. The avalanche was now a substantial wave of white, travelling with great momentum. With a scream of terror, Messner was torn from the slope and thrown towards the crevasse. Heavy, wet snow swamped him, pinning him down. He fought with maniacal strength to free himself from the awful blanket until he broke to the surface.

Lackner was ashen-faced and looked more shaken than Messner. "Are you all right? Are you injured?" was all he could say.

"Yes, I'm all right," Messner replied, shaking the snow out of his clothes and hair. "But I've lost my ice-axe." Wryly he thought to himself of the people who were always saying that it was essential for safety to climb with a companion. Did they realise, he wondered, that a companion could sometimes be the cause of an accident, however unwittingly?

It takes a jolt, a close brush with death, really to put the proper values of life into sharp focus, Messner reflected that evening as the sun cast a rich burning pallor over the Chamonix Aiguilles. Lionel Terray had talked about climbers as Conquistadors of the Useless, yet Conquistadors had been brave heroic fighters out to slay an enemy. In reality mountains were too solidly inanimate to be looked upon as an enemy. There were no ogres in the hills, no dragons to slay. Any wound a mountaineer received was entirely self-inflicted.

Mountaineering really was a joke, as ludicrous as the spectacle of Don Quixote tilting at a windmill, a huge joke with tiny, insignificant man waving an axe at a huge natural fortress. But if it was a joke, reflected Messner, that did not devalue the effort, the self-knowledge a climber could gain from seeing precisely how far the joke could be pushed. Many tens of thousands were attracted to mountains, climbed them and remained unharmed; but Messner was aware how many of the great mountaineers had died over the years, climbers who had pushed the joke to the ultimate point until it had rebounded on them. Terray himself, Bühl, Egger, Lehne, Couzy, Oggioni, Kinshofer, Harlin — the list went on, would go on. Many had died previously on climbs that he had now completed; come to grief on the very same patterns of holds and stretches of rock that were part of his experience.

The point of mountaineering was elusive and lay outside the material interests of normal, sensible conduct. If there was a risk he would have to take it. Whatever darker subconscious motives were now driving him, if indeed there were any such egocentric forces pushing him along, it was too late now to turn back. Climbing was dyed deeply into his nature and he was as committed to going forward as he would have been after starting an irreversible pitch.

The first solo assault during that season had been on the Civetta, a mountain that towers like a fortress wall above the small Italian town of Alleghe. A number of routes run up the formidable north-west flank of the mountain, few of them more severe than the Philipp-Flamm, named after Walter Philipp and Dieter Flamm of Vienna who pioneered the climb in 1957. None is more committing.

Messner disagreed with the purist school of mountaineers who believed that to be aesthetically right, a route should reverse the line taken by a raindrop falling from the top of the cliff. Such geometrically direct lines usually meant scarring the rock with bolt holes, but this was not the case with the Philipp-Flamm. The route runs in one elegant line from the foot of the huge cliff to the Punta Tissi. It climbs the gentler angled ribs forming a long sweep of flying buttresses to the face which then thrusts a row of perpendicular fingers seamed with fine cracks for 700 metres to the summit.

There is a beautiful symmetry to the cliff and a purity of line about the Philipp-Flamm which makes the route a natural target for any mountaineer who seeks to indulge in ultimate solo alpinism. Messner determined to attempt it.

By now his positive views were considered by some to be dogmatic. He was never afraid to say precisely what he thought about any mountaineering issue, however unpopular that made him. If this view was too uncomfortable for some Alpinists, reducing their achievements and suggesting that they should not be attempting the hardest routes if they needed so many artificial props, Messner never hesitated to express it. And there was no arguing with him. His qualification for standing in such solemn judgement on the achievements of his fellow mountaineers was the pulpit of his own experience. This was raised several metres by his attempt on the Philipp-Flamm during that spectacular summer of 1969.

The warden of the Tissi hut said nothing when Messner announced his plan, but his eyes spoke volumes. The man had seen some tough-looking climbers attempting the north-west wall of the Civetta in his time; departing from the hut in a clamour of ironmongery, rucksacks stuffed with rope and all kinds of protection. Many had come back with their tails between their legs after experiencing the problems beyond the foot of that awesome wall. Quite a few had not come back at all. Now here was this lanky, quietly determined man plainly announcing that not only was he going to climb the hardest route on the face, but he would do it solo.

The warden's expression told Messner that he considered him mad: that he was obsessed and would be offending the unwritten rules of mountain climbing.

Messner, however, felt superbly fit. It was a crisp summer morning and the sun was shining brilliantly. He felt composed and clear-minded. The part of his brain that calculated possibilities, that measured risk against experience, steepness against strength and stamina against fatigue, was coldly subdued. Climbing was entirely in the mind and he was firmly of a mind to climb the Philipp-Flamm. It was not bravado. He had been up the route four summers previously with Sepp and the sections of the climb were clearly imprinted in his memory.

Messner had stood at the foot of many mountain walls and looked up at many hundreds of steep climbs, picking out the grossly foreshortened route to the top; assessing the line and its difficulties, and judging the quality of the rock. There was a special exhilaration about this climb threading its spectacular path to the Punta Tissi. The wall consisted of acres of weather-wrinkled rock pitched vertically and set with the menacing shadows of small overlaps.

A light summer mist clung like rags to the towers above him. As so often, he could hear the calls of a party of climbers who had left the hut ahead of him. In his diary Messner noted that there were two groups ahead and the first was traversing to the foot of a dièdre in the centre of the face. The route followed a crack behind a huge block and the rock there was friable and made him uneasy. He moved after them with a quick rhythm up the rocks. The softer angle of the face at this point felt facile to a body keyed up for solitary combat. He overtook the second party, who turned out to be Czech climbers, and moved on to the stance from which the leading pair were making a thin traverse to the left. Messner waited there, uncoiling his rope and preparing to move off. The first Czechs allowed him to overtake them. Messner did so but his rope, running through a series of fixed pitons, snagged. When he asked the Czechs to free his rope there was an argument which disturbed his concentration. He made a number of false moves. His climbing lost some fluency. But this irritating grain of sand worked its way through the machinery until he was out of sight of the others and once more totally alone.

A fine haze of rain drifted across the rocks, then the shower strengthened. Messner, under an overhang, was protected; but looking down he saw the Czechs retreating. He was fully committed now with a drop of 700 metres below and a further 400 metres of extremely severe rock above — damp rock that was greased by rain, slabs that shone with a deadly polish. The rubber soles of his boots gained only a tentative grip on the rock. He felt terribly vulnerable. A crack came into sight and he swung into it, his back jammed against one wall, legs braced on the other. Automatically he moved up it to a point where an iron bolt secured one of the difficult parts of the climb. This ugly mark of the route's great popularity jarred on Messner. He pressed on, reaching the next crux beneath a huge roof that jutted out and blocked the route ahead.

He was only just managing to retain a cool, nerveless attitude and the idea of retreat was now in his mind. He could still have reached the foot of the cliff from here. From a higher point it would be very difficult. The rock was not only unpleasantly greasy but at that point it was stained with blood. The leader of a recent party had been struck by an avalanche of stones and had fallen off.

Messner arranged his self-belay, although the notion that he might actually part from the rock did not enter his mind. He moved out on tiny holds beneath the angle of the roof and over to its left-hand edge. There was another crack and he reached for holds to enter it. His fingers curled around good incuts and he felt the muscles in his arms and legs move with powerful coordination like a machine defeating the steady tug of gravity. Once in the crack he untied the self-belay, coiled the rope and slung it over his back. Then he continued. Eyes scanned the holds, calculated the moves. The nervous tension in these high reaches of the face was intense but each step was made with absolute precision and such confidence that the stark presence of a drop which had grown now to nearly 1,000 metres was reduced to a point of total irrelevance. More overhangs followed and more moves leftwards which he ducked like a boxer riding punches. He was over the slabs now and into the summit couloir which he reached with a certainty that there could be no retreat.

The final third of the face was the one most exposed to the weather. The rock was drenched and running with water, soaking Messner's clothes and trickling down his arms, chilling his body whenever he reached for holds. Paradoxically, he was desperately thirsty, dehydrated by the intense exercise of the climb.

The drop beneath him was obscured by a carpet of cloud as thick as a safety blanket. Occasional snowflakes mingled with the rain. He had to move to keep warm. From the couloir the great overhang of the Philipp-Flamm jutted out, the crux of the entire climb.

In *The Seventh Grade**, Messner recounts his experiences of this section of the route in sharp detail. "This is regarded," he says, "as the most difficult pitch on the climb and, recalling that some very good climbers had come to grief here in the past, I went hot all over as though fear had sharpened my perception.

"The next pitch was steep and as the rock was very brittle, the piton at the start came away in my hand. I knocked it in more firmly and tied it to another one which I inserted myself and used them as a belay. The climbing at this point was extremely severe, added to which I could only utilise the holds for pressure.

"I traversed to the right above the cave and reached a smooth and narrow crack. The rope had run out and as I tried to pull it up, it jammed. I pulled desperately at it with one hand while I held on to a flake with the other — it would not move. I swung the rope from side to side as far as my exposed stance would allow, pulled again, pulled until my left hand got cramp. This was dangerous, for strong fingers were essential for the next section of the climb, the summit couloir, more essential even than the perlon rope. Eventually I had to snap it through with the hammer and I was free. . . . It was hailing now, heavily and steadily, and my clothes were dripping. I was in the summit couloir in the middle of a waterfall. I gazed anxiously into the dark canyon above me — it was grey, slippery and full of hail. Suddenly I heard an explosion overhead: lightning had struck. I hugged the wall and stones whistled past me. My movements were intuitive, completely automatic. Only instinct acquired over many years of activity can save one in such dramatic situations. Step by step, I clambered up the waterfall. To be really up against it creates its own

* *The Seventh Grade* by Reinhold Messner, Kaye and Ward Ltd, 1974

terrors. There are many such ravines in the Dolomites, but for me there is only one like a strangler's hand.

"I did not want to admit to myself that I was frightened. 'Straddle, spread your legs out,' I said to myself. Then with unwonted calm I began to knock in a piton. The water splashed down between my legs.

"I was hoping to find shelter in a cave and frequently thought of a bivouac. But the cold was so intense that, after a short rest, I had to go on. I would never have withstood a night out under these wet and cold conditions, even in a bivouac sack. I had taken the precaution of stuffing my bivouac sack under my pullover before I left the hut, but I did not get it out because subconsciously I was still hoping that it would stop raining before nightfall."

It was fortunate for Messner that he could remember details of the route from the time he had climbed here with Sepp, although the conditions were very different now. Mist turned the rocks black, it was intensely cold and his clothes by this time were completely water-logged. His trousers felt so heavy that he feared they would fall ludicrously to his ankles so he took them off and tied them around his body. The daily cold showers at home were now paying dividends, since they had helped to prepare him for such a drenching. Even so, the muscular effort of his economical climbing barely created enough heat to keep him conscious. Instinctively he moved up the final steep holds, juddering with cold, soaked through.

When at last he stood on the summit of the Punta Tissi, his only gesture to mark the triumph was to haul on his sodden trousers. He then set off quickly down the easy descent, and warmth soon flooded back into his body.

At the Coldai Hut the warden gave him news of an approaching army of journalists. His young brother Werner was waiting there and Messner was beginning to feel the full impact of the climb.

"Please, you must wait and tell them your story," the warden said.

"Not now," Messner replied; "come, Werner, we must go home."

Chapter 6

THE TRAGEDY OF NANGA PARBAT

AFTER THE GOLDEN season in the summer of 1969, the thought of a life-style which he had not previously considered possible began to form in Messner's imagination. He was acknowledged to be a leading Alpinist. His record of difficult climbs and first ascents was unequalled. But few people so lacking in private means had launched out and earned a living as a professional mountaineer. More than a living, Messner sought to earn enough to explore the giant mountains outside the Alps. The trip to Yerupaja in the Andes had whetted his appetite for the bigger ranges. If he had set new standards in the Alps then surely that philosophy and tactical approach could be extended to the Himalayas. He did not let the publicity dampen his spirits or change his plans. He decided to lead life as he chose.

Günther, still his strongest climbing partner, had won his economics qualification and in the previous year, 1968, had begun working in a Bruneck bank. He disliked the orderly life and the restrictions, however, and admired Reinhold's freedom, particularly when Reinhold received an invitation from Dr Karl Herrligkoffer of the Deutsches Institut für Auslandforschung (DIA) to join the 1970 Sigi Löw Memorial Expedition to the south face of Nanga Parbat.

Here was a two-fold opportunity. Unlike Britain, where the Mount Everest Foundation gives assistance to individual expeditions, West Germany does not have a regular sponsoring body for mountaineering projects. Another system is the privately run DIA led by Dr Herrligkoffer, which organises expeditions that give young Continental climbers a chance to climb in ranges that would otherwise be impossible for them to reach. The face which the German team sought to climb was regarded at that time as the most difficult mountain wall in the world. It was four times as high as the Civetta, almost three times the height of the north wall of the Eiger and led to the summit of an 8,000-metre peak. So Messner naturally became very excited about the prospect, and began

72

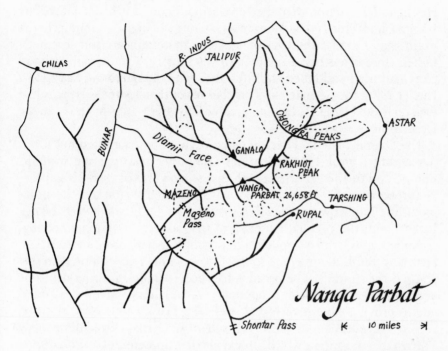

methodically to study the problems that would be entailed. In particular he read everything he could lay his hands on about climbing at altitude.

His talks with doctors who were experienced in high-altitude medicine were immensely useful and he began to form a picture of the so-called "death zone" a climber enters beyond 7,000 metres at which point physical deterioration is rapid. Messner calculated that his training, rather than being aimed to overcome technical difficulty, should be developed towards increasing stamina, strength and superlative fitness.

The expedition required considerable financial involvement from its members so Messner took a temporary job once again at the secondary school in Eppan, a pleasant spa town not far from Bolzano. He was a popular teacher there, taking classes in mathematics, physics and physical education and forever spicing his lessons with anecdotes about his climbing adventures. His mornings were devoted to the classroom, the afternoons to gruelling training sessions and a study of the climbing history of Nanga Parbat. It was not at all a happy history and the new expedition had a tinge of the macabre about it. Sigi Löw, in whose memory the attempt on the Rupal flank was to be made, had died eight years earlier after reaching the summit by the Diamir flank. Willi Merkl, who was

Herrligkoffer's stepbrother, died on the mountain in 1934 and altogether Nanga Parbat (the Naked Mountain), among the highest summits in the world, had claimed the lives of nineteen mountaineers and seventeen porters since it was first attempted in 1895. In 1932 a German-Austrian party had tried and failed and from that time the mountain had held a Lorelei allure for German climbers. No fewer than eleven Germans had died on it and Nanga Parbat had become known as "Destiny Peak" in the German newspapers.

The Diamir flank had been the first route to be attempted but it was not climbed until 1962 when Sigi Löw, after reaching the summit, unroped on the descent, fell on an easy section and cracked his skull.

Throughout the 1960s the Germans repeatedly attacked the peak, mounting four expeditions, all of them led by Dr Herrligkoffer. Nanga Parbat, with the peculiar nationalism that adheres to mountaineering, remained a "German" mountain although it had been an Austrian, Hermann Bühl, as a member of the 1953 German expedition who first reached the summit. The paradox had been paralleled earlier the same year on Everest, a "British" mountain, when Hillary, a New Zealander, and Tensing, a Sherpa of Nepal, were the first on top. Now Messner, a South Tyrolean, was to be the star of a German expedition on a "German" mountain which, to extend the nonsense of nationalism a little, might have been a "British" peak had A.F. Mummery succeeded in climbing it in 1895. Clearly, the closer national expeditions get to the summit the more international they may become!

When Mummery reached the upper part of the Diamir valley, he inspected the face through a spy-glass and picked out what appeared to be a natural line to the summit. It ran between overhangs of ice and up a section of sharp ridges of rock that were later named after him. Mummery and his Gurkha companion, Ragobir, reached the section of rock and climbed the central spur, a fine achievement in nailed boots and with simple Alpine equipment. Watching from the rocks above the valley were Mummery's two colleagues, Collie and Hastings. They saw the two climbers set up camp and carry stocks of food high on to the face. Storms swept over them yet still they persevered, reaching a second band of rocks above which an unstable slab of ice weighted with fresh snow lay poised.

Collie and Hastings saw the explosion of white powder as an avalanche billowed down the face. When the snow dust settled two figures emerged from the maelstrom and climbed stubbornly on. They were close to the summit ridge when they next came to a halt and after a short while turned back with Mummery helping his porter to descend. His plan was probably to make a bivouac camp at 7,000 metres and then try again when they had recovered. But it was not to be. More snow fell on the face leaving it covered with unsprung avalanches. Mummery, Ragobir and a second Gurkha moved from the Diamir face across a col joining it to the Rakhiot valley — from which Bühl climbed Nanga Parbat 58 years later.

Hastings and Collie walked into the Rakhiot valley and waited there while Mummery and the two Gurkhas traversed around the mountain across the Diamir Col. They never arrived and no trace of them was ever found. The assumption is that the fresh snow made the lower slopes of the mountain unsafe and the climbers perished in an avalanche.

For Messner this story, like the epic experiences of Mallory, Irvine, Norton and Odell on Everest, contained the lesson that, with determination, climbers could not only contemplate reaching these great altitudes but actually succeed in making it to the top. It must certainly be possible to do better than climbers who had persevered without benefit of modern down clothing; or even ice axes, twelve-point crampons and high altitude boots. So he began systematically working towards the Nanga Parbat attempt. He collected all the information he could about the mountain and examined photographs of the Rupal face minutely through his magnifying glass, memorising the features and trying to imagine what the difficulties would be like close up. Within the limits of the distorted perspective he reduced the climb to a series of technical moves. He also continued to read as much material as he could lay hands on about the physiology of high altitude climbing. He adopted the basic tenet that even the Himalayas could be seen as a series of technical moves and that the other objective hazards of size and altitude could be reduced by sheer hard training.

The Himalayas, he reasoned, required both physical and mental stamina — and these were perhaps even more important than technical proficiency. This was why he concentrated on running rather than on climbing, forcing himself daily to run up and down at least 1,000 metres, running on his toes until his calves and thighs felt as if they were on the point of bursting.

His experience in the Andes was helpful now, and he reckoned there were three points on which to concentrate to achieve the degree of endurance which Nanga Parbat would demand. The first objective could be reached by anyone who was reasonably fit: to be capable of half a day of solid exertion without feeling seriously tired. The second concerned storing up glycogen in the liver: he felt that he had built up a sufficient store after a number of big Alpine routes, when he was able to climb hard for six or seven hours without suffering substantial hunger or thirst. The final point was to be able to maintain the action of his liver and kidneys even in a state of extreme dehydration, and this Messner could only test on Nanga Parbat itself when he had to draw on his last reservoirs of strength.

The Andes adventure had shown him how an expedition to a big mountain should be organised, and how to adjust to the rhythm and routine of building camps and ferrying supplies up the mountain. Although he had not been to the Himalayas before, he felt immensely fit and kept to a fairly stringent diet. Once a week he restricted himself to a day of eating nothing but fruit. Before leaving for Nepal he also ate large quantities of garlic which did nothing for the bouquet of his breath but, according to a convincing medical article he had read, made the walls of his heart more supple.

The months slipped by and Messner began to revel in his four hours of daily exercise. He and Günther trained together, and over the Christmas of 1969 the two brothers, with two other companions, attempted to climb the north face of Monte Pelmo which at that season had the look of a gigantic wedding cake, it was so thickly plastered with snow. Twice on this 1,000-metre face the climbers bivouacked. They found that the famous water pitch was a funnel of green ice, and by the time they reached the final huge tiers of rock a snow-storm had put the face in a treacherous condition. Wisely, they abseiled back to the foot of Pelmo and were none the worse for such extremes. Messner felt reassured that his harsh training-routine was yielding results. The climb itself, which to many mountaineers would have been extremely arduous, had been straightforward and physically untaxing so that a correct decision to retreat was made rationally, without panic and well within safety bounds.

Some weeks before the expedition was due to leave for the Himalayas, an invitation arrived for Günther to join it. One member had withdrawn and Reinhold suggested that Günther should take his place. But his acceptance was a fateful decision.

Günther obtained leave from his job in the bank at Bruneck and in early March 1970 Reinhold came up from Padua. The whole family met for a farewell at their home in Villnöss. Everyone turned up — all nine children with their friends and relations. It was a tremendous send-off and father Messner proudly slapped his sons on the back and wished them good luck.

Frau Messner looked at them both. They were so strong and confident, but they were not simply going away for a few days into the local mountains as they had done so many hundreds of times before. They were going far beyond the Alps to the other side of the world to attempt the highest continuous face on earth, and one where many mountaineers had died. It was even a memorial expedition and its very title was a reminder of the dangers. She held her sons close before they left. "Be careful," she said, as she always did. She was never to see Günther again.

Messner took in the Rupal flank of Nanga Parbat. Its size — nearly 5,000 metres from bottom to top — was hard to comprehend immediately because his eyes adjusted to the scale and made it difficult to compare with any other mountain wall he had climbed. The sun lit up the gigantic features, snowfields towering in parallel lines towards a series of dark buttresses. He felt that he already knew practically every rib and corner.

The central pillar, jutting out from the main block of the face, was the route least likely to be threatened by avalanche; unfortunately, the technically easier sections lower down had areas that were clearly in the firing line from above. Of the four previous German expeditions to the Rupal face, none had reached closer than 1,000 metres from the summit, with the steepest part still to climb.

It was plain, looking at the mountain from Tap-Alp, that the objective dangers would be infinitely more severe than those of the Alps. On an Alpine wall the risks were more calculable: on most well-known routes they were downright familiar. There was the weather of course; that could always spin the roulette wheel, but the scale was such that, if his skill was sufficient, a really competent mountaineer could scuttle back to safety. Here it was different. In the centre of the Rupal wall of Nanga Parbat the most skilful climber was, to an appreciable extent, at risk from dangers quite outside his control that could not be predicted.

Nanga Parbat kept reminding the eleven climbers in the expedition why this great southern flank had never been conquered. Huge avalanches and stonefalls regularly swept down the face and, when bad weather settled in and made them invisible, their growling and crashing above base camp was even more sinister. The work of securing a route up the mountain and fixing camps went smoothly. The Messner brothers were responsible for siting some of the important camps on the face and Reinhold's preparatory work with his magnifying glass proved invaluable. Camp II, set at the angle where the Wieland Icefield joined the main pillar, was positioned under a 20-metre ice cliff above which avalanches were divided, sweeping by to left and right. The next camp, known as the Ice Dome, had the same kind of shield protecting it from the volatile mountain. The Messners climbed together all the time, sheltering for one period of ten days in the Ice Dome as a snowstorm lashed the face and slowly eroded the chances not only of climbing higher but also of safe retreat. Eventually there was a slight lull in the weather, the clouds thinned and weak sunlight raised the climbers' hopes. But the weather report from Peshawar remained gloomy. After so long at almost 7,300 metres it was becoming essential that they should return to base camp instead of pushing on to establish Camp V below the Merkl Icefield. On June 13 they came down and two days later everyone had returned to base camp. Hopes of reaching the summit diminished.

Reinhold and Günther had no wish to give up. They had both acclimatised well and had shown their fitness in a quick descent. Their supplies of food had to be conserved carefully and supplemented by yak meat slaughtered and butchered locally while, for more than a week, they waited at base camp until the weather improved. Finally the Messner brothers with three other climbers set out again, and so began one of the most controversial and tragic of mountaineering sagas.

By June 26 time was clearly running out, with the approach of the monsoon that would bring prolonged bad weather. The highest camp was still far below the summit and Reinhold suggested on the radio from Camp IV that he should make a solo bid for the top if the weather was going to be bad and speed was essential.

Previously, at noon on June 26, Reinhold had suggested to Herrligkoffer that he should climb to Camp V that same evening. Since he would be out of radio contact with base, a system of rocket signals was proposed. If the weather forecast was bad, a red rocket would be fired. If it was good, a blue rocket would be the signal. Blue and red fired together would indicate doubtful conditions leaving the climbers at Camp V to decide for themselves. Messner was clear in his mind that if a red rocket was fired from base camp, that was to indicate bad weather approaching and a solo attempt to secure the summit quickly before conditions made that impossible. Dr Herrligkoffer later denied that this had been the understanding.

The Messner brothers with Gerhard Baur started out for Camp V which other climbers had established the previous day. They were moving up the Merkl Icefield in darkness when at about 8 p.m. a red rocket soared into the sky from base camp. They waited for another but none came. All three continued to the assault camp and it was agreed that Reinhold would set out alone early the following morning.

At 2 a.m. Messner struggled out of the crowded tent. The moon lit the mountainside eerily and the sky was full of stars. His head-torch picked out the route to the foot of a chimney choked with powder snow. This was the famous Merkl Crack. He traversed away to the right but returned to his starting point when that proved too difficult. In the half-light of dawn he discovered an ill-defined ramp which led upwards and around the most difficult section of the Crack proper. The ramp was long, at least two pitches, but no harder than Grade Three and only partly covered in snow. Messner moved up it easily.

Daylight came and he rested, very satisfied with his achievement so far. The face was extremely steep and exposed but he was making good progress and he felt strong and not badly affected by the altitude even though he was now entering the death zone.

He was about to move on again when, glancing down the mountain, he saw Günther climbing out of the area of the Merkl Gully. His brother must have taken no more than four hours to climb the entire gully. Reinhold waited for Günther to reach him.

There were no explanations as to why Günther had decided to follow his brother's tracks up the mountainside and none demanded. Günther and Gerhard had fixed some rope at the foot of the Merkl Gully. Gerhard had retreated to Camp V with a sore throat, Günther had carried on. Neither brother had brought a rope.

It was early afternoon when they traversed under the south shoulder of the Rupal flank, the highest rock and ice face in the world. Rags of cloud billowed around them, occasionally allowing a view down into the Rupal valley. They could clearly see the Silver Plateau and Rakhiot Peak and Reinhold reflected that this was where Hermann Bühl, the first man to climb Nanga Parbat, had fought his own lonely battle for survival.

They moved to a gentle slope of hard wind-glazed snow which swung up to the summit. Günther looked radiantly content and shook Reinhold's hand warmly as they reached the highest point. There was no hint then of the fight for survival that was about to begin.

It was clear that the two climbers would not be able to return to Camp V before dark and that they would have to bivouac on the mountain. Reinhold made an inventory of their equipment. It was very short. A lot of thought had gone into getting up the mountain; rather less into getting down again. They retreated along an easy boulder ridge to a sheltering notch some 150 metres below the summit and overlooking their tracks leading up the Merkl Gully. Reinhold hoped that a descent into the gully from this point would be easier.

Günther was now beginning to suffer the combined effects of the high altitude and his tremendous exertions earlier in the day in catching up with his brother. He felt ill and exhausted and unable to reverse their route on the Rupal face without the aid of a rope.

The night, spent huddled together in the cold thin air at almost 8,000 metres, did not improve matters. In the morning he felt convinced that retreat down the Rupal face without a rope was impossible for him. At 10 a.m. Reinhold looked down the mountainside and was overjoyed to see two climbers moving slowly towards the upper section of the face. They were Felix Kuen and Peter Scholz. Help at last. The pair were roped together.

Then came a tragic misunderstanding in a shouted conversation between Reinhold and Felix Kuen. They were separated by 100 metres of mountainside swept by winds that made communication difficult. Messner shouted down to Kuen: "We want a rope!" Kuen waved back apparently in acknowledgement. There were garbled snatches of conversation but Reinhold gained the firm impression that help in the form of a rope was now definitely on the way.

Kuen's recollection of the conversation is quite different. When he returned to Base Camp, Kuen said he had asked Messner whether everything was okay and he had replied "Yes". Kuen admitted that this lifted a great weight from his mind. He had feared Messner was calling for help.

The Messner brothers sheltered in their high bivouac under the notch waiting for help and Kuen and Scholz continued on their way to the summit. The misunderstanding was complete. Within half an hour Reinhold realized that help was not on the way.

Even now there are unsatisfactory gaps in this story. Messner was clearly taking a very high risk in his solo attempt but could well have pulled it off had Günther not made his unexpected appearance — in spite of his singular lack of climbing or survival equipment for such a serious route. He had staked everything on being able to move quickly and when Günther had joined him this had reduced the assault to an inter-dependent partnership but with none of the security that a rope would normally have afforded.

It is surely unthinkable that Kuen deliberately left the Messner brothers to perish in their bivouac. Yet if the Messners had secretly planned, as has been suggested, a complete traverse they would hardly be sitting around doing nothing at 10 a.m. when they could by then have been far down the Diamir flank. The only reason why they could have been still so high on the mountain at that time of day was because they had run into problems and were waiting for help. And if that was the case, why would Messner shout down that everything was "okay"? From the muddle over the rockets, to Günther's impetuous decision to follow his brother and the few words exchanged on a mountain face, the saga of Nanga Parbat became a tragic series of misunderstandings.

There was only one more choice, the Diamir Face. During the winter they had studied Nanga Parbat intensively and read many books about the mountain so that they had a strong picture in their minds of the difficulties. This was now a great advantage. In one glance down he could see the curve of the basin and recognise features on the face. He could imagine the Mummery route, as he could recall a thousand other mountaineering lines in his head. The question for Mummery in 1895 had been whether he could succeed without technical aids and that dilemma was being repeated now.

Messner felt sure that Günther would recover further down the mountain where they could hope to get help from shepherds in the Diamir valley. Even so he was afraid of this descent into the unknown. Surely they were too experienced to be afraid? Perhaps the fear came from there being no other alternative. They would have to risk it. Around 11 a.m. they prepared to descend the Diamir side. It was a decision of life or death. They had no rope, and no other way out.

Reinhold made a final scan of the peak and then looked towards the Merkl Crack. There was no one there. The mountain was empty. His face was a mask of hopelessness. He said to Günther: "No point in waiting for them. We will start to climb down the snow slope over there." He pointed to a line of cornices far below them.

They had to find the best, the only possible way. Messner knew well that without a rope he would not be able to help Günther. He asked Günther: "Do you think we will be able to get round that block down there?"

"I think so." Reinhold looked at him and said: "We cannot be certain." Günther replied: "No, nothing is certain."

They continued the descent. They could not avoid a feeling of inevitability, but as they slowly picked their way down the face the conditions improved. Reinhold led the way, searching for the safest route. Occasionally he would stop and wait for Günther, who was not moving as fast. Beneath them a thunderstorm was spending itself. Once to the right and then to the left there were bright flashes of lightning followed by flurries of sleet, and then a heavier shower of hail swept the mountain. Clouds gathered in the Diamir valley, swirling about and making the downward route invisible. Soon the valley was completely blocked out by mist. The abyss was hidden, but it had to start somewhere. They could not see where. Suddenly the mist opened up like a dark hole. The wall plunged more than 2,000 metres into the Diamir valley. It was one of the most breathtaking sights Messner had seen but he had no time to admire it. He had to decide how they could escape from the steep maze.

Again Reinhold climbed down first so that he could study the openings in the layers of mist and find the way down. With any luck there would be a safe escape route. He waited again. Günther was far above him, hardly discernible in the mist. He descended slowly, carefully trying out each foothold. One mistake would be sufficient — only one mistake. On the steep wall each movement had to be thought out, carefully calculated. Perhaps subconsciously thought out.

Günther arrived beside him. "How are you feeling?" Reinhold asked. Günther did not reply but looked past him down the mountainside.

"How does it look?" he asked.

"It will be okay," Reinhold replied, giving his brother a careful look. He was clearly tired out but determined to get down, to survive.

Günther said he felt thirsty and Reinhold took a sherbet tablet from a tin in his pocket and handed it to him. He emptied the rest of the tablets into his pocket, scooped some snow into the tin and began breathing hard on the snow. Günther watched the operation keenly. After ten minutes a mouthful of water had appeared in the tin. Reinhold handed it to his brother who drank it, eyes closed in ecstasy as the liquid relieved his parched throat. It also bucked up his spirits and the two climbers continued their descent. Their escape route passed between two large serac zones and down towards a rib of rock which, when they reached it, turned out to be a wall of ice.

Their will to survive still burned strongly. Their descent of that treacherous face was made methodically in spite of their exhaustion. Reinhold still led the way, searching for the safest route, retracing hundreds of metres of height because an ice cliff blocked their way. Again where a rock step appeared too difficult for Günther in his weakened condition, the brothers turned back only to find an impassable crevasse barring the way.

The daylight died but the two brothers had descended to 6,500 metres. Surely they would be safe now with the worst of the difficulties behind them?

They spent a second night out on the mountain, shivering with exposure, gaining what little warmth they could from each other, unable to feel their feet, only a numb emptiness at the tips of their limbs. At dawn Günther felt a little better, drawing on his last reserves of strength, and they set off together towards the complex of glaciers that led into the Diamir valley.

Which way? Reinhold wondered. There was a choice of possible routes and Günther needed to conserve energy. The sunlight was already triggering avalanches on the face around them.

A sudden, sinister rattle of stones warned them that they were not yet safe. The glacier curled away into the distance like an old, dead tongue but beyond its tip they could see the start of the woodlands that grew up from the Diamir. They were both spent but they had almost completed the first traverse of an 8,000 metre peak.

"You could wait here," Reinhold said, observing the exhausted figure of his brother, "then follow on. I'll check the route down, that it's possible, and then you can follow."

Günther nodded agreement and sat slumped beside the glacier. Reinhold went ahead and found a safe route off the ice and waited for Günther. He barely registered the heavy crash of avalanches on the Diamir Face. Günther did not arrive. A slow, appalling fear stirred Reinhold. He climbed back on to the glacier and painfully made his way back to the point where he had left his brother. There was no sign of him, only the fresh scar of ice debris thickly strewn around the place where he had been, the broken splinters of seracs that had crashed down on to this place.

The awful truth was too great for Reinhold to grasp. He must be in the wrong spot, he thought desperately. Günther must be somewhere else. Perhaps he had stumbled off in another direction.

Such terrible apprehension filled Reinhold that he searched the glacier with a frantic energy. All caution deserted him. His clothing was torn, his feet became wet and then iced over. The truth that Günther had been killed slowly entered the core of his consciousness. He was numbed, then desolate. He waited on the glacier for help but no one came. Slowly his feet and body froze. The agony of thirst, exhaustion and pain in his limbs tortured him. He stumbled automatically down to the valley. Unable to walk he eventually crawled on all fours, more dead than alive, delirious yet still forcing his thin, pain-wracked body to keep moving.

He reached a small meadow where two men came to help him. They took him to a nearby village and gave him food. Reinhold pulled his boots from his frost-bitten feet and fell asleep, exhausted. When he woke next day his feet were terribly swollen and his valuables had been stolen. He cut branches from a tree and made two improvised crutches and then hobbled to the next village where he found help. Reinhold had survived but he was tortured now by pain and the awful knowledge that his brother was dead.

Chapter 7

REQUIEM FOR A BROTHER

THROUGH THE WINDOW of a ward on the tenth floor of Innsbruck University Hospital, Messner was aware of mountains towering over the city's rooftops — not a hostile wilderness like Nanga Parbat, but the gentler, more companionable summits of his familiar Alps. He lay against the pillow and looked down at the neat bandages covering his feet. They made his limbs seem club-like. At the end of the bed, a chart marked the amputations. Left foot, toes one to four; right foot, toes one and two; all partly or entirely removed. Oddly, beneath the bandages he could sense that his feet were still whole. His blackened fingers too were bandaged and painful but were responding to treatment. They would be saved, so the doctors said.

His haggard features still reflected his ordeal. His face was thin and drawn. First there had been Günther's death and the shock which that had brought to the whole family. He and Günther had climbed hundreds of mountains together, often by extremely difficult routes. There had been moments of real danger but always by skill and speed they had escaped. Never had Messner felt that their sport was seriously threatening their lives. Then there was his own mutilation. Would he still be able to climb well? Would his tolerance of severe cold be affected, would his balance be destroyed? There was no telling until he tried but there had been the quiet assumption in his mother's eyes that this, surely, would be the end of his days as a serious mountaineer.

Reinhold lay immobile in bed for more than a month while his feet healed. He had not questioned to himself the series of decisions he and Günther had taken on Nanga Parbat which had led to the accident. After all they had almost made it safely into the Diamir valley. It was an avalanche that had killed Günther, not a failure to cope with the technical problems they had encountered on that side of the mountain.

Messner was angry then when *Bunte Illustrierte* carried an article, a world exclusive, written by Karl Herrligkoffer, the expedition leader, in which he said that Günther "seemed to all of us to be too weak for the summit." The maelstrom of controversy which was to rage over the expedition thereafter was already building up.

Reinhold replied with his account of what had happened on the first summit attempt and also prepared to publish a book, *Red Rocket on Nanga Parbat*, giving an even fuller account of the tragic traverse of the mountain. He maintained that before his attempt on the summit he had spoken by radio to Dr Herrligkoffer before he left Camp IV and arranged that if the weather forecast picked up on the main radio at base camp was good, a blue rocket would be fired. A bad forecast would be signalled by a red rocket. Messner also maintained that a red rocket would give him the signal for a solo attempt in order to bring the expedition to a swift conclusion. He insists that this arrangement was approved by Dr Herrligkoffer. If the forecast required a blue rocket, then it was agreed that there should be a conventional, roped attempt which would take longer but would be safer. This arrangement was made because there was no direct radio communication between base camp and Camp V, the camp below the summit.

On June 27 when a red rocket was fired, the plan for a solo attempt was embarked upon. Later in the wrangle Herrligkoffer said that the radio conversation had been distorted by atmospheric conditions but several times, he said, he had recapped on the meaning of the rocket colours. No attempt had been agreed upon, he said. In *Alpinismus* he wrote: "In no circumstances could I agree to a solo attempt on the summit in menacing bad weather, with its attendant unusually increased risks."

The row became increasingly bitter with accusations from Messner about the search and rescue facilities provided by the expedition, and about premature removal of camps on the Rupal Flank.

Herrligkoffer replied with injunctions, writs and denials. Messner's book, *Red Rocket on Nanga Parbat*, was banned from being distributed on the grounds that he had signed an agreement with the expedition giving all the rights of anything written or published about it to the DIA. The culmination of all these claims and counter-claims was a judgement in the Munich Landgericht on September 16, 1975. The eventual cost to Messner of the time-consuming legal battle (he had been pinned down by a strong contract with the expedition) was some 50,000 DM.

After leaving hospital, there was plenty to distract him. He had another book to complete (on the story of Alpinism), and lecture tours to arrange about Nanga Parbat and Grade VI climbing. On July 18 a requiem mass was held for Günther in the Church of St. Peter, Villnöss. The building was full, the atmosphere solemn. Reinhold sat among the congregation, his feet still bandaged, sensing strongly, in the formal ceremony, the permanence of his family's loss. Günther, the gentle, self-effacing man was dead and this seemed to Reinhold a terrible, empty waste. He could accept the abstract idea of death; could even apply it to himself as part of the inevitable risk of mountaineering, but the reality applied to Günther was desolating. It was one thing to consider the objective dangers and the theoretical possibility of being killed, quite another to accept the elimination of someone so close beneath the irrational crush of a million or more tons of avalanching mountainside.

Günther had been keen to accept the challenge of Nanga Parbat. He had been as strong an Alpinist as Reinhold, as fit and as quick on difficult ground, but because Reinhold was by eighteen months the older and therefore the more responsible brother, he had generally taken the position of leader.

Günther had climbed with other friends and with them had himself led some of the most difficult routes in the Alps but his partnership with Reinhold had always been the most rewarding. Perhaps if they had both survived Nanga Parbat they would have gone on to attempt more difficult Himalayan routes together. But it was useless to reflect on what might have been. The brutal fact was that of those who attempted the most difficult feats in the sport of mountaineering, only half survived to look back on their climbing careers from the stance of old age. The rest died.

The wake of grief, mutilation and law suits with Dr Herrligkoffer was not all that followed the tragedy. Some newspaper reports even suggested that Reinhold had left his brother to die on the mountain. Added to the personal loss, this weight of innuendo was hard for Reinhold and his family to tolerate and as daunting in its own way as the ascent of Nanga Parbat. The traverse of what for years had been the ultimate mountain to the Germans was marred, not only by the accident, but by the subsequent controversy. This ghastly series of misunderstandings, with snatches of conversation torn away by the wind, had left Kuen convinced that the Messner brothers did not need help, and Reinhold filled with relief that help was now on the way.

From the Messners' point of view two things had been sure: Günther's certainty that he could not descend the Rupal flank without a rope and their knowledge that the Diamir flank was less steep and therefore possibly less difficult. For Reinhold the argument rested upon the, for him, indisputable fact that he had intended to make a solo attempt on the summit and had not intended that Günther should go with him. He also insisted — and continues to insist — that Dr Herrligkoffer knew of his intention, which Dr Herrligkoffer, equally positively, denies. There, after a host of statements and counter-statements and the legal action which Messner lost, the Nanga Parbat affair rests.

Messner had argued that by hard training, by schooling his body to resist the obvious menace of cold and altitude and by moving swiftly over dangerous ground, a climber could reduce the objective dangers. He was convinced that the sheer will to survive was absolutely decisive and might even influence objective dangers. "I am not saying," he once wrote, "that a man's will can stop rocks breaking away or hinder the passage of avalanches." But if a man "knew himself" and was in "real contact with himself and his surroundings" he was less likely to find himself in the path of an avalanche or crumbling serac. He placed his faith, therefore, in a profoundly subtle instinct that reduced the likelihood of finding himself in such a position, and now he carried this idea a stage further.

He concluded that he had survived Nanga Parbat through being driven by an overwhelming desire to live. For all that, death would certainly have been easier than the experience he had survived. He was no longer afraid of the prospect of death, but the immediate effect of the tragedy on Nanga Parbat was to leave him feeling ill and vulnerable. It was at this time that he entered into one of the stormiest but most significant relationships in his life.

The plane from Delhi had touched down at Munich airport with members of the Nanga Parbat expedition on board. The door opened and Messner felt with a shock the cool air of a different continent — so different from the dust, heat and the pungent smells of Kathmandu. The families of the climbers milled around the arrival lounge. The room was noisy with the excited clamour of reunion. The climbers were easy to distinguish: lean, deeply sun-tanned and full of the adventure. Reporters and photographers were keen to interview Messner. He waited in a wheel chair, aware of the pain from his heavily bandaged feet. Baron Max Engelhard von Kienlin, one of the team, pushed through a group of photographers and called out: "Reinhold, please meet my wife, Uschi."

Messner saw a slim, dark-haired woman next to Max, smiling at him. He nodded briefly at her but his mind was too occupied with the thought of meeting his own family, of explaining Günther's death and worrying about his own health to notice more about Max's wife. He was wheeled out of the lounge to where an ambulance waited to take him to Innsbruck.

Uschi came to see him in hospital. She was vital, open-natured and full

Above: Josef Messner as a student

Right: Reinhold Messner as a
young man with his mother

Left: Helmut,
Reinhold, Günther,
Erich, Siegfried and
Hubert Messner as
children

The family holiday hut in the Geisler Alps

Above left: Geisler Alps: Saas Rigas – Reinhold's first mountain

Above right: The church wall at St Peter's, Villnöss: climbing "school" for beginners

Günther Messner in 1969

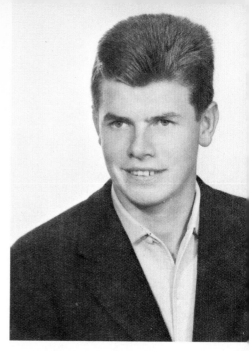

Reinhold Messner in the early 1960s

One of the first climbs with Günther

Winning the greasy pole contest

Above: Climbing free on the north face of the Sassolungo

Left: With Heinrich Messner after climbing the Furchetta north face

After the north pillar of the Eiger. Günther on left

Yerupaja

Right: On the summit of Yerupaja

Below: In the Dolomites

Above: The Diamir face of Nanga Parbat

Left: After Nanga Parbat

of energy, not what Messner expected of a German baroness who lived in a *Schloss*, had two young children and was expecting a third.

Uschi explained that her father-in-law had been a mountaineer. Max, her husband, was born in 1934, the same year as the tragedy on Nanga Parbat in which Willi Merkl had died. He had become fascinated by the history of the mountain. He was only six years old when he first read about the fatal attraction it had for German climbers and even as a boy he had dreamt of seeing it. When the chance had come for him to join the Herrligkoffer expedition, for a fee, Uschi had encouraged him to go — to fulfil his dream.

Quickly Messner realised that there was a gulf between Max, the formal, although very friendly German aristocrat and his high-spirited independently-minded wife who disliked the rigid style of German high society. Her hope was that an adventure on Nanga Parbat would widen Max's outlook. Messner had an immediate, instinctive liking for Uschi but he did not consider then that their friendship would deepen. Despite her different character, she seemed content with her marriage to Max. It was ridiculous to think that she would give up such a grand life-style, her children and security to live with someone who made a profession out of proving the impossible possible, who spent so much of his life on such a dangerous edge.

However, they met often and Messner visited the von Kienlins at their home. He felt a growing tension in the marriage and understood Uschi's unhappiness. Over the following year his relationship with her strengthened and Uschi became an invaluable prop in the legal wrangles over Nanga Parbat, the press conferences, the negotiations with publishers and the flood of inquiries that someone so much in the public eye is subjected to. The wake of the Nanga Parbat expedition grew more and more angry. Some newspapers repeated the slur that Messner had left Günther to die on the mountain and when the romance between Uschi and Messner was eventually sniffed out, Reinhold's notoriety grew even further. In August 1971 Uschi divorced under bitter circumstances and joined Reinhold's restless life.

This step was taken one year after the return from Nanga Parbat, and it marked the end of a tempestuous period. Reinhold's feet had healed well and he quickly became accustomed to the loss of several of his toes. Fortunately the damage from frostbite was not bad enough to affect his balance. In the spring of 1971 he and Uschi went back to the Diamir valley. They camped in the place where less than a year before Messner had crawled out of the glacier more dead than alive. He went up to the foot of the face and searched for any signs of Günther — sometimes a glacier will disgorge what lies buried in its slowly moving stream. But he found nothing.

Revisiting this place naturally reminded him of his psychological scars but Messner felt completely recovered physically. The furore over Nanga Parbat still lingered but he firmly decided that his life would continue to be devoted to mountaineering. It was a simple formula: he would try to go one step beyond the "threshold" with each of his expeditions and when he succeeded would tell everyone about it in books and lectures. It would be a lonely and precarious path, in financial as well as mountaineering terms, but Uschi was now there to help to organise the practical details. It was also clear from the reaction to the events on Nanga Parbat that people had a great appetite for personal accounts of such adventures and all he had to do was to retain the public's interest through the quality of his achievements.

Reflecting on his climbing career, he did not expect that the traverse of Nanga Parbat would be judged by history as too significant. It had been an arbitrary response to a crisis, unlike Bühl's first ascent of the mountain which had been planned. But its private effect upon himself was significant. He and Günther had survived from one minute to the next, beyond the limit of physical and mental endurance. There had been no dramatic fear of dying, only a numb acceptance that they might not survive and, imposed upon it, a tenacious will to endure. That experience, Messner felt, had made him a different person. The boy whose retribution was extreme when wrongly attacked had become a more rational man, able to see more clearly the real value in people and in his own resources, and able to shrug his shoulders when the rumours about him became poisonous. On the sound platform of his relationship with Uschi he could rest firm and assured. He had had few girlfriends, although men who performed such extraordinary climbing feats generally attracted girls as nectar does bees. But he had never allowed anyone to become totally important to himself. Now this slim, dark and cheerful woman, so resilient and spirited, really was extremely important to him.

Surely, he thought, he could never be so important to her? There was already so much in Uschi's life and she had strong ambitions herself. The experience of being trapped in the stultifying limbo of German high society had made her determined not to slip into another conventional union. Reinhold would continue climbing his mountains and she would lead her own life. Logically, someone who lived continually on the lip of disaster must die at some point, merely on the law of averages, but she felt positive that he would not be killed. The longer he persisted, surely, the more suicidal it became, yet to Uschi that never seemed true. She knew that the more mountains Reinhold climbed the more experienced he became and the more alert he was to those subtle differences in himself and on the mountain that could be fatal.

Because Uschi was of German nationality it was easier for her to obtain a divorce from Max in Germany than if they had both been Italian. In the summer of 1972 she and Reinhold were married at a civil ceremony in Villnöss, to the disapproval of local folk who were devoutly Roman Catholic. Although Messner would have been happy simply for them to live together, he ignored the disapproval and bought a large house at St. Magdalena in the next village up from St. Peter. The building had once been a school but the trouble of converting it was more than rewarded by the superb view directly down the Villnöss valley.

Reinhold then began acting as a guide in Villnöss and founded a climbing school with Heinrich Messner, his former climbing companion who was a local farmer.

He wrote continuously, frustrated by the way *Red Rocket on Nanga Parbat*, which could otherwise have been a bestseller, had been prevented from reaching the bookshops by Dr Herrligkoffer's injunction. He had already proved that he was a proficient photographer, too, and he concentrated on further improving his skill. Perhaps the future lay partly in that direction.

Chapter 8

MANASLU — A COSTLY VICTORY

MESSNER BEGAN CONSIDERING what lay in the long-term future and how he could keep his adventures both sensational enough, and satisfying to his own growth as a mountaineer. Alpine climbing had gone through three phases. At first it had been necessary only to reach the summit; then Alpinists had concentrated on reaching the summit by the most difficult route and not caring too much how that was achieved; and now style was the ultimate aim — avoiding the use of too many pegs, eschewing expansion bolts and making it a sporting contest between man and mountain.

Surely the same would happen in the Himalayas, with climbers adapting Alpine methods to the highest peaks, as he and Günther had inadvertently done on Nanga Parbat? Then there was the possibility of solo ascents in the Himalayas, an ultimately dangerous endeavour when all the risks of distance, altitude and sheer scale were added together. Would he dare to try it? Or would it be left to the next generation of climbers to push on to that further stage?

Administration was difficult enough. Obtaining permission to climb the routes was an extremely trying process. Foreign expeditions were an important source of income to the authorities in the countries that happened to have high mountain ranges and the foothills of Nepalese and Pakistani bureaucracy were as forbidding in their way as the hardest of mountains.

For as long as anyone locally could remember, the Himalayan peaks had been sterile ground, nothing but a source of danger and a cradle for mythology. But now teams of westerners arrived and, for no reason the locals could understand, sought to climb the inaccessible peaks not only by the traditional ways but by the quick direct lines. In a strictly commercial sense, men such as Messner were bad for business. Far better to have the long files of pale and panting trekkers wandering along the trade routes from Pokhara and into Solo Khumbu. They brought more than these lean ascetics who moved faster than even the locals could go and who had strange ambitions to climb the great peaks alone — something which only the winds and the more solitary gods were properly allowed to do.

By 1972 Messner's name was commercially attractive enough in Europe to command substantial backing for expeditions he organised himself or that he joined. While Uschi helped to run his life, ensuring a full diary of lectures, interviews and meetings with commercial contacts, he developed his own future plans, applying for permission to tackle new peaks. Most of his income was ploughed back into the "business" but he was developing an excellent relationship with the large Munich publishing house of BLV. A number of photo-journals throughout Europe were also keen to publish the spectacularly illustrated adventure stories that he was able to tell. He was ambitious and aimed to climb as many 8,000 metre peaks in the world as he could, developing a type of small, swift-moving expedition that was both comparatively cheap and satisfying to take part in.

The next opportunity to tackle a major Himalayan peak came with an invitation to join the 1972 Austrian expedition to Manaslu in the Gurka Himal, a giant among giants and the world's tenth highest mountain. It had been climbed fewer than half a dozen times and had repulsed many more attempts. The summit rose from an angled ice-plateau which could be reached from a number of directions. The huge tectonic thrust that pushed this young ridge over 8,000 metres above sea level also created the summits of Himalchuli and Peak 29 to the south and the neighbouring ridge that contained the multi-headed summit of Annapurna.

The expedition fielded a strong team. The climbers knew one another and got on well. "Wolfi" Nairz directed the climb with unobtrusive style and Messner found himself greatly enjoying the slow, integrated campaign to ascend the difficult mountain. All went smoothly throughout the month of April, and a third camp was established at 6,300 metres on the south-west saddle. Camp IV, 1,100 metres higher, was reached in two stages by climbing an ice ramp quite as complex as some entire Alpine routes. The summit attempt could be mounted from this camp during the last week of April.

The weather had been superb for a long spell allowing all the camps to be well stocked. Everything ran with ideal smoothness; Horst Fankhauser and Andi Schlick climbed towards Camp IV ready to support the first attempt on the summit. Jurg Hochfilzer and Hans Hofer, who had worked hard building up the camps, returned to base to recuperate. Wolfi, Josel Knoll and Sirdar Urkien went to Camp III and by April 25 all was ready, with the weather still settled and snow conditions excellent.

At Camp IV Franz Jaeger and Messner started out in the early morning for the summit, some 700 metres above them. Their crampons bit easily into the hard snow and they moved quickly over the straightforward ground, a broad plateau which began to seem interminable. At each new rise they expected to see the summit, only to be confronted by yet another shoulder reflecting the blinding sunshine. The two climbers did not rope up. There were no crevasses or technical difficulties. The snow was in perfect condition and the sky empty of any hints of a storm. It was impossible to imagine that the stage was set for disaster.

At mid-morning Franz Jaeger caught up with Messner just as Manaslu had presented them with another couple of unexpected slopes under the summit. The ground ahead was steeper and he declared that he doubted whether he could both make the summit and descend in one day. The thin air was making him feel tired and he had absolutely no wish to be caught out in a bivouac at nearly 8,000 metres. Messner looked around. To the north there was no sign of cloud, only the peaks in Tibet standing out sharply, perhaps too sharply. The view to the south was blocked by the ridge.

The two climbers assessed the position. Messner felt in splendid form, unaffected by the altitude and not at all stretched. Franz, too, was in good physical shape, only concerned that the altitude could prevent him from reaching the top and back. He decided to turn back but had no wish to prevent Messner continuing with the summit bid. Neither had any reason to think that Franz, who was properly equipped, would not arrive safely at the camp alone. The ground was so easy that they had not bothered to rope up.

"I'll be waiting at Camp IV with some hot tea for you," he promised Messner.

"Fine," Reinhold replied. "I don't know how long this will take but I should not be more than a couple of hours or so behind you."

The two men parted. Franz Jaeger retraced their steps down the plateau, Messner turned to the two steeper slopes of hard snow that led on to the summit ridge. They were broken by sentinel gendarmes which made the climbing rather more difficult beneath the actual summit, but then came the last rock pinnacle, and finally that curious sense of unfolding distance that comes on the summit of a giant peak. Suddenly he was there.

Directly beneath the summit rocks the Japanese had left two pegs and a flag which the wind had reduced to a tattered rag. Messner looked around the horizon. To the north the sky was still clear but the southern view, which had been obscured by the ridge, was alarming. Banks of thick cloud were billowing towards Manaslu and already the wind was rising beyond the steady blast which had greeted him when he stepped out of the shelter of the ridge. It was a positive warning to return and Messner heeded it immediately.

Within minutes the descent became a battle for survival as the storm broke around him. At least Franz would by now be in the safety of Camp IV, Messner thought, as he wiped the snow from his face before it iced up his features. He moved painfully down through a wild blizzard, forcing himself not to give way to panic. It was hard. A distinctive ice slope reappeared in the wind-blown spindrift and he knew he had wandered in a circle. The wind built up to hurricane level and Messner huddled before it, fighting not to be blown away by its strength.

He became extremely anxious about falling. Although the ground was not difficult, once he began sliding out of control in his smooth nylon windproofs he knew he would stand no chance. His clothing would be transformed into a death sledge because it provided no friction. Deliberately he tore the material with the point of his ice axe. That would create more resistance against the slope, he thought. The wind seemed to be striking him from all directions. He could get no general indication of direction from it. Visibility was nil, blocked off by the screaming, hooligan gusts which whipped up spindrift that choked his nose and mouth, suffocating him.

Messner had struggled down the mountain and supposed himself to be within a radius of at the most 500 metres from the camp. Even more demoralising, he occasionally heard someone shouting to him through that featureless grey wilderness, but he could find no sign of the tent. He had been battling through the blizzard now for hours and slowly realised that he was completely lost and would not be able to survive alone for much longer in such conditions. He was alive, aware and still quite strong but he could see his life draining irrevocably away from him.

Only when the wind died slightly could he hear the calls. Messner shouted back to Franz but could not get any help. He stopped wandering around in circles and huddled down in the snow, forcing his frozen brain to think. In clearing the snow from his face he had clawed at his skin and beard, tearing out lumps of hair in his frantic attempt to breathe, so his cheeks and nose were covered in dried or frozen blood. His lips were cracked and parched, and dehydration had given him a raging thirst. He noticed that the grey obscuring cloud was growing darker and more dense and realised with dumb horror that night was falling. He could see no way of surviving now. He sank miserably into the snow. The wind eased a little. Messner forced himself to move. Some deep, buried instinct for survival compelled him to his feet. Dimly he struggled for the glimmerings of an idea that might save him.

That was it, the wind; that was the key. Now that it had lessened to merely a strong gale screaming across the plateau he could sense its steady direction. Gales on Manaslu always came from the south. Walk into the wind and unless this particular gale was a maverick, he would hit the south face. The tent, he knew, was pitched on the plateau just by the exit from this face. It stood at right angles to the wind direction and on each side of it he remembered seeing buttresses of rock, the only rocks on that stark plateau. If he could find them, the tent must lie in between. It was the only hope left and he stumbled on. Suddenly he stopped short where the edge of the ridge fell into the void of the south face. He turned at right angles and worked his way carefully along the edge, eyes straining into the mist. Something solid appeared ahead. It was one of the buttresses. He turned and walked at ninety degrees, guided by the wind, until the second buttress appeared. He covered that trail four times before he stumbled on the tent. Mighty relief flooded through him and as he called out a figure emerged in front of him. It was Horst Fankhauser. To Messner's horror he realised that Franz Jaeger was not in the tent. Only Horst and Andi Schlick were there. Messner was now exhausted and collapsed in the tent. The relief of finding it released the tension and the drive for survival that had kept him going.

He could not rationally argue with Horst and Andi when they decided to look for Franz. First Horst left the tent and returned, then both of them set out along the gentle slope of the plateau in the howling whiteness, hoping to find the missing man. They headed in the direction of the route but the wind was now building up again, battering the summit of Manaslu.

Horst and Andi too were now lost and conditions were growing worse. Their only hope was to dig a snowhole and sit out the storm. Meanwhile, Messner kept leaving the tent and shouting into the storm in the hope that the others would hear. There was nothing, only the scream of the wind.

Andi and Horst were in fact not so far away. Although they had dug a shelter they decided to quit its doubtful protection and try to locate the tent. But the storm was too fierce for them. It was impossible to see anything in the blinding wind and within minutes they again became completely lost. They dug a second shelter and huddled there, both frozen now and seriously threatened with the mutilation of frostbite. They massaged each other's limbs and fought to stay awake and not drift away into a slumber that would lead gently into death. Eventually Andi announced he would leave the snowhole and see if the weather was improving. He struggled through the entrance, leaving Horst huddled miserably inside. How long had they been there? Hours, perhaps, but they felt like days.

The wind continued to shriek across the bare flanks of Manaslu. Horst had the impression that outside their hastily-dug shelter there was some raging maniac. How could the wind scream so? What chance did Franz have in such terrible cold? Would he, like them, be crouched in some hole perhaps only a few metres away, hiding from this ogre of a storm? Like them? But Horst was alone. Slowly it crept into his numbed brain that Andi had not yet returned. How long had he been gone? Horst struggled to look at his watch but gave up. There was no point in that. He tried to measure the frozen, miserable minutes since his companion had left the shelter. Panic sent a recharging surge of adrenalin into his system. Anxiously he peered out from the entrance and called Andi's name. His voice was whipped away from his lips and smothered by the storm.

He struggled out of the hole and began to search for his companion on the ridge. Keeping his back to the brunt of the storm he searched as best he could. It was impossible. Never had he known such an alien place. He stood in the wild gloom calling Andi's name but even if his friend had been immediately beside him he would not have heard. Dimly he hoped his voice might carry down the wind and be picked up by Andi or Franz. Now the cold began to bite right through him. He felt the deadness where circulation could no longer force a way through frozen tissue. There was nothing more he could do and if he stood where he was he would simply die achieving nothing. So he crept back to the snowhole, praying fiercely that the others too had found somewhere to shelter. At the first hint of dawn he struggled to the surface and was able to pick up his bearings. He climbed through deep fresh snow to the site of the tent and dug down to it.

"Reinhold, are you there? Is Andi with you?"

A figure stirred in the tent and Reinhold's face, haggard with exhaustion, appeared.

"No one came," he said.

"God, but Andi left last night and didn't come back. He was gone for ages and I tried to find him but there was no sign. We must look for him and Franz. They must have dug shelters. They must be here somewhere."

Reinhold marvelled at Horst's strength and determination. He struggled out of his sleeping bag and the two men left the tent and went out on to the plateau.

The storm had died and a wide area of the desolate mountainside became visible. Snow had fallen heavily and lay in chest-deep drifts. Slowly, they had to accept that since neither of their friends had appeared, it was likely that neither had survived the night. Unless they had dug a shelter, in such a storm at such an altitude and in such deep cold it would have been impossible to stay alive. They searched the ridge for any signs of their friends until a fresh blast of wind warned them that another storm was brewing. The clouds boiled down the side of Manaslu.

"It's getting bad again; there is nothing we can do here," Messner said. Both men were exhausted.

"We can't expect that anyone will be able to get up to us. The snow is so deep, the avalanche risk must be high below the plateau."

"That's true. We must get down."

Shattered and depressed they forced a route down to Camp III where Josel Knoll greeted them and heard their story with horror. Both Reinhold and Horst could sense the symptoms of frostbite in their hands and feet. They rested and immediately went on down to Camp II where Dr Ölz treated them with inter-arterial injections to get the circulation flowing to hands and feet once more. The pain was intense and added to the mental misery of the loss of their two comrades.

Snow continued to fall for several days, creating an even greater avalanche danger between Camps III and IV. Daily it became even more impossible for search parties to hope to reach the plateau. Dejectedly the climbers descended to Base Camp.

Messner again felt the numbing sense of loss and anger. He knew with certainty that there was nothing that he or Horst could have done. Both were amazingly lucky to escape. When Messner had stumbled into the tent he had been more dead than alive. It was beyond the bounds of physical possibility that he could have gone out immediately to search for Franz.

Was he right, he asked himself, to have separated from him below the summit? Perhaps, with hindsight, they should have stayed together. But that was the kind of decision that mountains demanded and which sometimes went unpredictably wrong. Franz had been feeling fit when he turned back. He had had no doubts that he would have been able to reach the summit, only whether he would have been able to get back to Camp IV that night. He was not as exceptionally strong as Messner and might not have been able to keep up with him on the descent. Franz had not wanted to force Messner into an unnecessary bivouac at more than 7,000 metres. He had decided to turn back when he was still feeling strong, when conditions were good and when there was only easy ground between himself and shelter.

At the time it had been a sensible plan, and the appalling storm building up behind the ridge had caught them unawares. However sure Messner was in his own mind that his actions had been reasonable at the time, there was certainly criticism when the expedition returned to Austria. Questions were asked in the climbing world about why he had not remained with Franz Jaeger when he had decided to turn back. If they had realised the state of the weather, would Messner still have pushed on to the top by himself? If the two climbers had stayed together then perhaps they would have found the tent at Camp IV in time and if they had done that, Andi and Horst would not have had to set out on their tragic rescue attempt.

At one time Messner would have become furiously angry at such accusations. But after Nanga Parbat, Günther's death and the law suit, he had grown to realise that mountaineering had two distinct sides: the real one of sweat, fear and intense exhilaration and the public one according to which climbing was viewed as an abstract adventure — a tableau in which the characters played set rôles and individuals like himself came under intense critical scrutiny from those who could never know the full story because they were not there. Who else, for instance, could really understand the frightening power of that storm or the effort of fighting to remain alive when the easiest thing would have been to drift into a cold, comfortable death?

After the shock of this experience, all Messner wanted now was Uschi, Villnöss and the time to consider, to write — and, eventually, to think about his next mountain.

Chapter 9

ACONCAGUA

BY 1973, MESSNER again had a firm idea of the direction in which his climbing career should be heading. The mountain walls he attempted next must ideally have the same ability to kindle the imagination of the growing number who took an interest in his adventures. This was not such an easy condition to fulfil since the field was quite competitive and there were other climbers around who were equally keen to tackle any problems that remained unsolved.

An obvious candidate lay in the remote mountain chain of the Andes, immediately beneath the highest summit of Aconcagua (6,959 metres). The south face of the mountain, a broad, weather-beaten wall more than 3,000 metres high, is broken by huge bands of rock, each band overhung by a frowning brow of ice. For years the face had been considered by everyone who examined it closely to be quite unclimbable. In the mid 1930s when Alpine climbers were locked in competition for the last of the major north faces in Europe, a Polish expedition reached the top of Aconcagua from the east. Much earlier, the mountain had first been climbed by its weakest line in January 1897 by Matthias Zurbriggen, the Swiss guide.

When European mountaineers began to apply their Nordwand techniques and experience to the highest peaks of the Himalayas and the Karakoram, Aconcagua's huge southern flank joined the list of possibilities. In 1954, one year after the first ascents of Everest and Nanga Parbat, a small French expedition led by René Ferlet attacked the face, following as close as possible the line of a pillar that bulged away from the main sweep of the cliff. They noted with keen misgivings that the cliff itself was constantly bombarded by stonefalls and avalanches from the belts of ice that appeared to extend across its whole width. The French team took a week for its final assault and was almost swept from the summit by a bad storm. In the 1960s two Argentinians climbed the face, but avoided the main buttress. And in the same year an international group of climbers tried another variation of the French line, avoiding many of the severe pitches but adding radically to the objective dangers with a long traverse beneath a high buttress of sandstone two-thirds of the way up. Two Japanese and one Spanish expedition also repeated the French route.

Messner's aim in 1973/4 was a new one. He intended to iron out the two deviations in the original route and to follow a smooth, direct line up the face. The South Tyrol Andean Expedition which he led offered the highest face in the New World as an exciting prospect to the young climbers of Bolzano. It was joined by Jochen Gruber and Jörgl Mayr who were both in the South Tyrol Alpine Club and had climbed with Messner on the Marmolata, Monte Pelmo and on the north face of the Furchetta; Konrad Renzler, a skilful mountaineer from the Pustertal, and Ernst Pertl, the well-known film-maker, who were also former climbing companions; and last but far from least by Dr Oswald Ölz, a fine mountaineer well versed in high altitude medicine. Known because of his strength, determination and manner as "Bulle" (the Bull), Oswald Ölz had been on the Manaslu expedition two years previously. Ruth Ölz and Uschi also went out with the team which arrived in Buenos Aires in late December, sorted out supplies, and then left on the 700-mile road trip to Mendoza.

Like nearly all mountaineering expeditions they were following the standard decelerating pattern. First there is a swift, almost supersonic flight; then a long, bumpy, dust-bedevilled journey by truck, slowing down further to the belligerent pace of a pack mule; and then the final, infinitely slow progress up steep rock and ice which eventually comes to a full stop, hopefully on the summit. It is as though a gigantic brake is applied to the mountaineers, grinding down their progress the nearer they come to their goal.

It was at dusk and by torchlight that the climbers in Messner's team finally reached Base Camp, two days' march from the military outpost of Puenta del Inca. They set up their tents in a sheltered hollow and the following morning woke in bright sunshine to see the 3,050 metre wall of Aconcagua towering above their camp. A brisk wind swept ragged clouds across the huge mountain giving an impression of busy movement — but it was not the only movement on the face. Regularly there was the brittle explosion of an avalanche breaking free, though on closer examination it appeared that the paths taken by the debris ran down either side of the main nose of the buttress.

By January 10 the climbers were prepared to tackle the face. An abortive start directly up the buttress drove them back to the French route, but then they made quick progress, fixing the ropes and abseiling back down to Base Camp. This was not maintained, however. On some days the wall was bathed in sunshine, on others Aconcagua had its head buried in the clouds and avalanches charged like tears of anger down the south face. On bad days the climbers consolidated the sections they had already climbed and took supplies of ropes to the latest camp. When the belts of high pressure swept across the Andes, they pushed on, fixing ropes to give an easy and well-secured route up the mountain. When Messner and Gruber reached the foot of the rock band barring the way to a great icefield, they found rock pitches that were occasionally grade six.

On January 16 Messner and Gruber settled into Camp I perched like an eagle's eyrie above the sweep of cliffs. As if they were guards changing on some high battlement they moved into the little tent while Ernst and Bulle, Jörgl and Konrad returned to Base Camp for a rest. They had pushed the route further and carried stocks of food and rope to supply the exploration of the central section of the face. The next day Messner led the way up the shattered section above the first camp, past the skeletal remains of a Japanese camp and out across the wide icefield. By noon they reached a high buttress which had obviously been foreshortened when viewed from Base Camp. From where they now stood, it rose with the sheerness of a Dolomite wall.

Messner again pushed the route up the most promising weakness in the rock, hammering one piton after the next into the deep sandstone cracks. In less than four hours the wall was beneath them and Messner turned his attention to a bulging mass of ice immediately above the rock. "Enough for today," he declared, and screwed home a large ice peg from which the pair could abseil, picking up the spider's trail of fixed ropes down to Camp I. Bulle was waiting there, ready to tackle the ice bulge with Messner the following day.

Gruber abseiled down the face leaving the two climbers at Camp I and the following morning he watched them through the telescope slowly working their way up on to the top glacier. In the afternoon the clouds gathered, swirling about the face, their upper edges full of movement, a sign that the wind had increased sharply. The stories of Aconcagua told of a white wind, the Viento Blanco, which froze everything in its path; a deadly, all-penetrating frost which a climber had little hope of surviving. On the ice bulge, Messner and Bulle both had an inkling that they might be feeling the first freezing breath of the Viento Blanco. The temperature had plunged and the wind was blasting flurries of fresh snow across the face. Occasional flickers of lightning brushed the ice with a hostile pallor. The two climbers opted to retreat and by dusk were safely down at Base Camp.

The storm delayed the expedition's progress but, unpredictable as ever, the sun shone on January 19. Mayr and Gruber walked over the wintry landscape to the start of the fixed ropes and climbed up, rucksacks bulging with provisions and equipment. The next day they moved on to Camp II and saw Messner climbing behind them, coming up direct from Base Camp.

Two days later Messner and Gruber continued to the final band of rocks and investigated the likely problems between them and the summit. Because they had only 60 metres of rope, they were obliged to return to Camp II to await fresh supplies. Gruber then started to show symptoms of altitude sickness. His throat ached and his head throbbed and within hours it was clear he would have to be evacuated to a lower camp. Bulle arrived with Renzler and administered pain-killers. The next day the doctor and Mayr helped Gruber to Base Camp whilst Messner remained on the mountain deciding what to do next.

The problem was a distinct shortage of supplies to support any prolonged summit bid. If the climbers became pinned down by a spell of bad weather their position would be serious. It seemed that the only alternative to giving up altogether, because time was also becoming short, would be to make one fast summit bid from the highest camp they had managed to establish.

Mayr had climbed back to Messner from his rescue mission and heard the plan. It was a long way for one push, he thought, and the band of rock above them did not look any too easy.

The next day, January 23, before the first pale wash of dawn had reached their camp, Messner and Mayr set out up the steep snow and ice slopes below the summit wall. It was loose and dangerous ground and roped together the two men made only slow progress. Mayr was now feeling the full effects of the thin air and slowed down, gasping for breath every few steps.

At the top of the crumbling rock band, Messner stopped and looked at his partner.

"How do you feel?" he asked.

"Not well. I can't catch my breath. The altitude," Mayr replied. He looked and felt miserable.

"We're not going to make it at this speed," Messner said. He glanced at his altimeter which read 6,380 metres. It had taken them about four hours to climb 400 metres and they were still 600 metres below the summit.

"If I go on alone would you wait here safe on this ledge until I come back? It will take about five hours, I guess.''

Mayr nodded agreement. It was a compromise, the only way for the expedition to succeed, but he felt disappointed. He watched Messner moving up over the broken ground; his steps were very positive and confident. As Mayr watched, resting, his strength returned. From the way that Messner was now covering the ground, it must be easy. Perhaps he would feel better if he reached a little higher. He would try.

Mayr untied the belay and moved off the ledge, following the indents in the hard snow made by Messner who was now 60 metres above him, moving strongly for the summit ridge.

Messner leaned on his axe and looked down the face. Mist swirled about the flank of Aconcagua but in the breaks of visibility he saw that Mayr had started to follow him and was steadily moving up his steps. Messner had just climbed a section of steep ice covered in an unpleasant sugary crust where he would have been happier to have a rope. It was very tricky ground and no place for Mayr to be alone and in his weakened condition.

He waited until Mayr was within shouting distance and then called to him, telling him to go back, and prepared himself to descend and call off the summit attempt if he refused. The mist became thicker and the wind that was buffeting across the slope grew stronger, whipping up a fine spindrift from the ice and flinging it into Messner's face in stinging flurries.

The dark figure paused and then began to retreat to the ledge. Messner watched for a minute and then turned back to the steep slope, hammering in his crampon points with as steady a rhythm as he could muster and moving upwards towards a convex bulge in the face which hid the Guanaco Ridge.

He had not realised quite how sheltered the south face was. The wind, as his head emerged over the edge of the ridge, almost plucked him from his holds. The warning signs of cloud and a fine spume of snow being torn across the knife-sharp edge betrayed the full strength of the blast. He retreated to the relative peace of the south face and armed himself against the Viento Blanco — for this surely was the demon snorting only a little way above his head. He pulled out over-trousers and a second anorak from his rucksack and put them on. A thick balaclava was wrenched over the fur cap he wore. Finally, he put on down mittens and ski goggles and then returned to the ridge. The cold did not bite so hard this time but the wind was as powerful as ever, tearing at him with a jetstream of ice.

According to his altimeter, Messner was only a few metres below the summit. He braced himself against the blast and struggled along the ridge, moving from one castellation to the next, seeking as much shelter behind the blocks as possible. It seemed an utterly lonely and hostile place so he was amazed to notice suddenly, moving down a gully below him, the figure of a man picking his way down from the summit ridge and moving painfully slowly, supporting himself with two ski sticks and taking awkward, club-footed steps down the broad gully. Beyond, below even the clouds that were boiling around the lower slopes, Messner thought he could see the bright dots of a cluster of tents. But there he was, a man alive in this life-forsaken place.

That live figure made the shock of finding a dead body even more acute. It lay below the crest of the ridge, clothes torn to ribbons by the wind, staring sightlessly into the valley, a stiff bundle that was on the point of becoming as much a part of the mountain as the rock itself.

The sight disturbed Messner, underlining his own vulnerable position. But he forced himself back to the practical business of reaching the summit and moved away along the ridge. There had been stories, he recalled, of a Japanese climber who had died near the top and who still lay there.

The summit cross was of aluminium, projecting from a heap of stones and bent by the wind. Nearby was a metal box containing scraps of paper left by those who had succeeded in reaching this point. He tore open a film pack and wrote inside: "First direct ascent of Aconcagua South Face, South Tyrol Andean Expedition 1974 on 23 January 1974."

The formality was complete but there remained the descent which would be far from easy. The cold was numbing. It slowed his thought and reaction to a series of tired gestures. His movements were automatic and he hardly registered the harsh rasp of the loose rocks on the summit ridge as he moved over them, the wild billowing of clouds against the Guanaco Ridge. He found the exit on to the south face marked by a notch that he particularly remembered. Once over the edge and out of the full blast of the wind, he felt the pain in his features as the blood forced its way back to the surface layers of skin. He became more sharply aware of his surroundings and began carefully to reverse the route. It was difficult because either the gusts of wind had erased his tracks or the ice was so hard that his crampons and axe had barely scratched the surface on the way up. There were few tell-tale marks to reassure him that he was on the right route. Cloud swirling around him and freshly fallen snow added to the difficulties.

Then he saw Jörgl Mayr, grinning at him from the shelter of his ledge. They were both extremely relieved to see one another. Messner had taken almost exactly five hours to reach the summit and return.

Snow was falling heavily now, adding to the risks. They reached the fixed ropes and began the familiar series of abseils down the precipitous face. Messner bounded down the rock walls, his legs acting as buffers, pushing his body out into space over the 2,000 metre drop. He saw flashing past him the sections of the route that had taken so long to climb. Now they were problems past, resuming their rôles as obstacles awaiting the next climbers who decided to attempt the face.

Mayr, with the impetus of action to stir and warm his body, quickly recovered his strength as they rappelled over the walls of rock and ice. They were spurred on by a constant cold trickle of fresh snow showering down the face and occasionally swelling into a powder avalanche which penetrated their clothing and made them nervous that a weightier fall might soon occur.

Suddenly the face curved out to form a gentle slope. They were on the scree and the dead ice of the glacier at the foot of Aconcagua's south wall. They were safe and within minutes, hands clasped around mugs of hot tea, they were ready to celebrate.

Chapter 10

MAKALU — A TACTICAL RETREAT

WOLFGANG NAIRZ WAS an ambitious but cheerful climber. Tall, wirily built and with soulful, grey eyes, he was not among the "tigers" of the Austrian climbing world but his even nature and conscientious ability to organise an expedition, calmly weathering even the frustrations which the Nepalese authorities could produce, made him the ideal leader. In 1974 he organised a team of ten climbers from the South Tyrol to attempt the steep and treacherous south face of Makalu, at 8,470 metres the fifth highest summit in the world. This was known to be a demanding climb from the tragic experiences of a Yugoslav party two years earlier.

Basically, the expedition was formed from the survivors of the Manaslu epic. For Messner that experience had been shattering but he had become hardened, and had contained his grief. After Nanga Parbat he had felt that nothing more could seriously touch him but Manaslu had nevertheless reached deep into the core of his consciousness. His chief consolation was that in that cold zone of death above 7,000 metres every man was equally at risk. It could easily have been his own life that was lost. Instinct, luck and a powerful drive to survive had saved him. It was a lottery in which he had some slight control over the result. The infinitely subtle ability to manage objective threats that came from repeatedly facing the same old odds, the same grey death-rattle of avalanche and freezing wind. He had been lucky but the more he practised, the luckier he became.

Now the same old race was on again on a different course. Makalu this time, the most handsome of the 8,000 metre peaks in Nepal, a fine, evenly-shaped pyramid of sharp ridges. First climbed by the French (Terray and Couzy) in 1955, the south face had a complex knot of glazed rock forming the upper half and a dark rock band, like a diagonal brush-stroke, stretching across the entire face at half height.

The expedition worked smoothly towards its goal and in three weeks had reached beyond the 7,000 metre mark with three high camps firmly established. Everyone felt optimistic and it seemed a question not of whether the summit would be reached but by how many of them. Above the third camp the route lay across bands of ice-glazed rock, steep but perfectly feasible.

Then the weather broke. How those first fine tendrils of high cloud, like blind fingers feeling their way across the sky, could change the attitude of an expedition! The temperature fell, the brittle sunlight died and the grey armour of heavy cloud came shouldering its way up the valleys. Hail rattled in fitful gusts on the ice, the wind rose from a whisper to a quarrelsome chatter against the tent fabric, then to a howl like some spectral hound. After the first barrage came a calmer spell filled with snowflakes; massive, downy crystals that stirred like dandelion seeds but settled heavily on the route of the climb.

The front of stormy weather passed and the next day revealed the face plastered with fresh snow. In the east, heavy cloud lay solidly in the valleys. The light slanting through the clouds struck the scattered summits below Camp III with splashes of rich colour: golds and yellows and, where the shadows spread, a cold translucent blue.

Camp III was an impressive place. Two Whillans boxes had been set up on a narrow ledge hacked out of a 50-degree ice slope, pinned there very thoroughly so that avalanches that swept down the face after each new fall of snow simply tumbled over them without doing any damage. It seemed immediately a crazy place to set up a camp, rather like stopping in the middle of a climbing pitch and burrowing into the slope, but in fact it was the safest place available.

On May 4 Messner and Gerhard Markl struggled out of their airy tents on to the narrow corridor joining them, clearing the snow that had fallen during the night which made the camp part of the slope again. Behind the east ridge of Makalu small puffs of heavy cloud threatened further snow before the day was out. Gerhard also noted a single cloud enveloping the summit of Baruntse. Both climbers felt uneasy but tried not to appear so as they strapped on their crampons and shouldered their sacks. The climb up the fixed rope began with the first step out of the camp.

Messner led off, kicking his crampon points through the covering of loose snow. At the first movement on the slope, small powdery avalanches were triggered off and fell down the steep face, dissolving in clouds of dust. The face higher up became more broken, with sections of very steep rock. Without the ropes that had been fixed in the previous spell of good weather the two climbers would not have been able to move so quickly. They climbed, 30 metres apart, not thinking about what was likely to happen when the fixed ropes ended and the real climbing began again.

A band of rock under the surface scraped harshly at the crampon points. The automatic movement continued, from one step to the next: foot, foot, axe, jumar; sliding it up the rope, and back to the feet again. The higher they reached the more difficult the climb became. The third camp now looked no more than a scratch on the mountain wall 500 metres below the climbers. Messner stopped to rest and looked down at the muffled figure of Gerhard climbing steadily up behind him. Then he moved on again. Gerhard could hear the regular intake of breath and see the slow, powerful movement of his partner above him. They climbed on until suddenly there was no more rope, no convenient protection up the face as they reached the place where the end was tied into a peg at the highest point.

Messner dug out the bunch of pegs, karabiners and the stout axe that Helli Hagner had left hanging there ten days earlier and clipped them on to his climbing harness. Gerhard arrived at the belay and looked enquiringly at the wall above and then at Reinhold. The two climbers began to feel uneasy, but decided to try to go a little way further.

With Gerhard belayed, Messner began clearing snow and moved up the rock which was barely visible. After 30 metres he thankfully banged a peg into a crack, hearing it ring solidly home, and tied on. Gerhard followed and looked around him even more uneasily. Above hung a remnant of white rope left by the Yugoslav expedition which had attempted the face eighteen months before. They had doubtless been lucky to find the face dry and free from snow in the fine, post-monsoon weather, but bad storms in the late autumn had caused their final assault to fail.

Their rope, a dubious-looking length of 7mm. perlon, dangled down enticingly on the otherwise empty face. It looked rather more bruised than the shreds of rope further down but the temptation to use it was great. Trying not to think too much about the damage that eighteen months of flogging in the wind could do to artificial fibres, Messner pulled on the rope and, with all his weight on it, banged home another peg. Tugging at the old rope again from the security of the belay, Messner could feel there was some elasticity remaining in it so, being cautious not to rely on the old rope entirely, he moved up and quickly covered another 20 metres of the rock band above, and brought up Gerhard.

They now stood on a narrow, snow-covered ledge with the wall rearing steeply above them. There were only two possibilities: a move to the right over snowed-up holds leading to unpromising ground, or a line directly up a crack, with some small holds, towards a distinct break in the steepness of the face. Messner moved off to the right but did not get far. He returned to the crack which was choked with snow. Two moves on fist jams, an uncomfortable technique in those conditions, and he hung there. The concentration on climbing had been so intense that he had hardly noticed the clouds which were gathering round them. He could just make out Gerhard's outline as he huddled on the belay, guarding the rope. Then snow began to fall.

"There is not much sense in going on with this," the grey figure below him observed.

Messner eased the lower fist from the crack and applied it higher into the cold fissure, clenching the knuckles so that it expanded and jammed there, holding his weight. "Just one pitch more," he replied, hauling himself up and hammering another peg into a crack. At least he was now firmly belayed but he seriously doubted that they would get much further up the face.

A long rightwards traverse over another smooth sweep of rocks took over half an hour and brought them scarcely 30 metres closer to the summit. However, this would do for another camp site, Messner thought, as he secured the rope to a couple of pegs. Soon they should be able to open the route to the fifth and final camp. At 7,500 metres they were less than 1,000 metres from the top. "A few more days should do it," he told Gerhard as they descended the fixed ropes.

But it was not to be. The next day fresh snow again covered the face making conditions extremely dangerous. It was impossible to clear the ropes and ferry the equipment up to Camp IV. The climbers even considered abandoning the face climb and attempting the normal route instead, but then they rejected the idea. A final attempt to make height on the face failed, and on May 9 they decided to break off the expedition. Snow had fallen again during the night and kept on falling for another week. All the preparation and effort had failed simply because an unpredictable pattern of bad weather had chanced to drift in at the wrong time.

At the foot of the mountain a pig had been slaughtered to celebrate success. It tasted just as good in defeat, the pork sliced into thin strips and grilled on sticks of bamboo. The expedition was coming to a close but Messner felt philosophical about the retreat. The experience was the important thing; not only the climbing, including that hard section taken on jammed fists, but the whole event of living for 50 days in one small close community bound together by a single endeavour.

Messner ran his eye over the base camp shelter with its smoke-blackened tarpaulin roof and the stones of the fireplace that were cooling now as the fire died and the Sherpas prepared to withdraw into the valley. It was a lonely and a dying place. The busy huddle of porters round the kitchen tent had gone, the chatter of the Sherpas — back down from carrying loads to the upper camps — that had become an integral part of expedition life was no more.

To the Sherpas, Messner reflected, the expedition had been little more than a job. Seventy-five pence a day for dangerous work. They enjoyed it. The pay was high by Nepalese standards. The price of an average Mercedes would make a villager in Nepal an extremely rich man, comfortable for the rest of his days. The Sherpas did not feel any regret at having failed to climb the mountain. They were inclined to shrug their shoulders and celebrate whatever happened. Life was certainly simpler that way, Messner reflected. Again it seemed to him that mountaineering was a joke — but a serious joke.

Messner wrote in his diary that he could not understand their failure. There was no reason for such slow progress above Camp III. Perhaps it had been the experience on Manaslu that restrained him when conditions became difficult and the storms had begun. Somehow the attempt had lacked conviction. This feeling was barely definable but could ultimately be measured in metres gained on the mountain. They had started out so convinced they would succeed and had seen the wall in such good condition that, when the storms arrived and the rocks became armoured with ice, the contrast and disappointment had made it an utterly hostile and impossible climb.

Chapter 11

RECORD TIME ON THE EIGER

NO ALPINE WALL held such a forbidding reputation as the North Face of the Eiger. In the 1930s when it became almost a parade ground for German National Socialism, young German climbers pushed well beyond the bounds of prudence attempting to win the wall and the Führer's approval. From the earliest attempts, the complex face, so threatened by storm and avalanche, claimed many lives.

The fact that Kleine Scheidegg and its hotel provided a comfortable grandstand from which to watch the life and death struggles actually taking place, added to the notoriety of the Eiger. Over the years people were able to view the frozen corpses of climbers suspended from ropes and, through the powerful glasses and telescopes that were perpetually aimed at the huge face, pick out the grisly trails of flesh and blood.

The Eigerwand became even more famous after a series of dramatic rescue attempts, and it held its grim place among the major Alpine walls for more than 40 years. It was a natural target for any climber of Messner's reputation, although he did not relish the clearly exceptional degree of objective danger. As one Eigerwander put it, "you can be the most gifted and confident climber in the world but if a stone hits you, that's it"; and on the Eiger the barrage of stonefall is a constant danger.

The fearsome reputation of the Eigerwand continued even though the new levels of skill, technique and equipment were being applied to it. In August 1963 Michel Darbellay, a young Valais guide, completed the wall solo using speed to outflank the objective dangers. By 1965 more than 140 Alpinists had climbed the Eigerwand and the following winter the final geometric progression of forcing a direct line up the face was achieved by a strong Anglo-American team who joined up with a German group of climbers with the same objective. The leading figure behind this direttissima was John Harlin, an American mountaineer who had climbed the face three years previously and had become obsessed with the idea of taking a direct line. In the attempt Harlin fell and was killed but the climb went on and the route was completed.

The old ogre still had its reputation, though, and Messner and Peter Habeler had nursed an ambition to climb it for eight years. But always the conditions were bad when both were free and good when one or other of them unavailable.

In fact Messner had twice already attempted the wall. During the summer of 1969, the season of so many other achievements, he tried to climb it with Erich Lackner but they were driven away from Grindelwald by miserable weather; then Messner returned alone. Conditions were at last good and he set out up the face, beginning the climb at night when the huge expanses of rock and ice were silver with moonlight. At least until dawn the route would be free from stonefall dislodged by the sun although there were one or two avalanches started accidentally by other parties on the face above him. It was one thing, Messner thought, to be alone on a great north wall, setting yourself against the dangers of staying on the rock or ice and finding the correct route. It was quite another to be bombarded by avalanches triggered by other climbers. A fusillade of stones, singing with menace as they hurtled through the air, descended in the darkness close by. With great regret he decided therefore that the enterprise was not worth the risk. He silently congratulated Darbellay on his solo ascent and retreated.

Nevertheless, he recognised that the face would normally be a perfect one for a solo effort with long, open pitches never reaching the sixth grade, but just a constant standard of challenge and, in the back of the mind, a reputation unlike that of any other mountain.

This brief foray on the Eiger rather defused any further ambition and it was not until 1974 that Messner and Habeler resolved to try again. Both climbers were now seeing the wall in a different perspective. Messner particularly had the experience of Nanga Parbat behind him as well as the Aconcagua south face. In his mind the scale of the Eiger had been reduced, and also the successful passage of so many climbers up the wall had taken the edge off its reputation.

It took three visits to Grindelwald that summer before the two friends considered that conditions were right. Twice they arrived and the face was drenched and totally inhospitable. Then in August, the weather forecast predicted a solid bar of high pressure settling over the Alps. On the 14th Messner and Habeler were at the foot of the famous climb again. The rocks were wet and they could tell by the slow progress of three parties already on the face that conditions were not good. A film company making the thriller *The Eiger Sanction* was waiting for better weather at Kleine Scheidegg with Dougal Haston, a principal star of the direttissima route up the Eigerwand. He had suggested holding on for a couple of days until the anticipated front bringing fine weather had actually materialised.

The two climbers decided to go at least to the start of the climb and reconnoitre. Messner's last attempt had ended at the Difficult Crack, but this time conditions were greatly improved. They crossed in the darkness to where the steep scree gave way to rock, but it was still not light enough to start the climb proper. There was no moon and the lights of Grindelwald shone up at them like grounded stars. They felt confident: the Eigerwand, a black shadow engulfed in darkness behind them, did not seem to have the menace of a mountain with such a dramatic and tragic history.

Habeler glanced up over his shoulder at the looming shadow, waiting for the first faint brushstrokes of light that would mark the dawn. He blinked into the darkness and nudged Messner huddled next to him.

"Look, Reinhold, up there — a torch flashing. I think it was once every half minute. Let's time it." Brightly, in the darkness, they recognised the international distress code; someone was in trouble. But should they raise the alarm or save time and go immediately to give help? They had ample rope and a full selection of pitons and wedges. Their medical kit was well stocked. They had plenty of food. Probably the distress signal would have been seen down in the valley 1,000 metres below them. To descend might waste vital hours; they had enough equipment between them to rescue any casualties through the window in the mountain wall made for the Jungfrau railway which runs through a tunnel in the Eiger.

In the first faint light of dawn the two men scrambled over the loose rocks at the foot of the climb. Above them the tiny pinpoint of light still blinked faintly high on the face. It was 5 o'clock. The lights of the hotel were coming on as they reached the steeper rocks; technically this was still easy ground but dangerously loose. Messner already knew this section of the route as it slanted up in a wavering diagonal line towards Difficult Crack. Beyond that point, at about one-third height, the Eigerwand reared its head and turned nasty.

They moved up the shattered face quickly with a cold dawn wind and concern about what might be happening above to drive them on. At the foot of Difficult Crack they sorted out their large collection of karabiners and pegs for both rock and ice, clipping them to their climbing harnesses. It was a wordless ritual performed at the start of so many climbs. A rope ran up the Crack, fixed there by the film crew, and soon Messner and Habeler had reached the Hinterstoisser Traverse. Water draining down the face coated the rock with a menacing black slime. Beneath the bottom lip of the traverse there was an almost sheer drop directly into the pastures of Alpiglen.

Messner led off across the traverse, moving neatly and quickly over the incut holds. A debris of old ice and shale led to a long sweep of slabs.

He compared what he saw with the mental notes he had made of the route. There was no time to be overawed by the gigantic wall. The surest way of defeating the Eigerwand was with speed. His eyes took in the dark oppressive brows of wet rock and picked out the signs of earlier attempts. A rusty piton hammered into a crack here and there, a few shreds of old rope. There were occasional cascades of water which saturated their clothing; Messner felt it soak through to his skin. Still, better to be showered by water than bombarded with rocks. Habeler climbed up to him, gave him a bleak grin and moved into the lead, running out a rope's length over fractured rock and fissures packed with ice. The second icefield now rose beyond them above a vertical rock step. They could see its cold lower lip.

One final rock pitch brought them closer to the edge of the ice and here at a corner they reached their objective, two Polish climbers crouched in a bivouac. They were exhausted and in difficulty. One had a broken leg, the result of a fall the previous day. Peter, in the lead at that point, offered help either by further medication or by organising a rescue through the ''window''. The two Poles declined; the helicopter would soon come, one of them said. Their signals had been answered from below.

They were right. Shortly afterwards the clatter of rotor blades could be heard and they saw the aircraft clawing its way up the huge face. It was a daring rescue. The noise and downdraught loosened rocks. Messner and Habeler were obliged to crouch in shelter as the missiles whanged past. The crew worked skilfully, close to the face: the Eigerwand was quite capable of sending down its own salvoes into the blades of the helicopter. As the machine inched closer, a man appeared dangling on a cable that was winched from the fuselage. He landed on the face and the machine tilted itself clear. The rescuer splinted the broken leg and the helicopter returned, lowering its cable again to the mountain like a slender proboscis. The injured climber, in a harness now, was lifted clear and the aircraft swerved away from the mountain wall. Within minutes the casualty would be in hospital and the helicopter would return for the others. It was a different story from the early days of the Eigerwand when climbers who were injured or trapped by storms had simply frozen to death.

Messner and Habeler strapped on their crampons now and launched themselves directly up the second icefield to its upper rim where a towering wall of rock shielded them from the worst of the stonefall. They had moved quickly up the ice on the front points of their crampons; how many climbers had been caught out on that second icefield traversing diagonally upwards from one step hacked out of the ice to the next? All the time they would have been vulnerable to the volleys of stonefall as the sun melted the ice on the upper reaches of the face and sent a continual shower which pitted and scarred the second icefield.

Fortunately it was a cold day, with the frost extending down to 3,400 metres so that the sunshine would have to work hard to release the normal barrage of debris.

The famous features of the Eigerwand were reached and overcome with quick precision. It was still early when they climbed through the Flatiron and up leftwards to the Death Bivouac. They felt in excellent form although the grim atmosphere of the sunless lower face kept both climbers on edge. In this area, Messner reflected, it would be suicidal to climb if sunlight was catching the upper limits of the face and sending down a solid Niagara of stones.

Shortly before 9 a.m., only four hours after their dawn start, the two climbers traversed from the last icefield to the severe rocks of the Ramp. Just above them, an Austrian quartet who had already spent four days on the face were clambering doggedly on. Peter Habeler knew the climbers and greeted them. They were happy to let him and Messner overtake.

Beyond the Ramp, boilerplate slabs of ice led to a steep pitch and a shattered crack which gave on to the Traverse of the Gods. Again they led through, which was quickest and prevented either of them from becoming too chilled. Their "waterproof" clothes were still damp from their early-morning drenching and clung to their bodies.

At noon they entered the White Spider, a high snowfield that sent tendrils of ice in all directions like the threads of a white web. The sun was still obscured by the bulk of the summit and the rocks gleamed with verglas. The Exit Cracks were choked with ice and the last sections of the face looked impregnable. On a ledge above the Spider they discussed whether to wait for the sun to move round and clear away the ice from the rocks or to continue immediately in more difficult conditions but without the threat of serious avalanche. They decided to move on and turned to the summit wall which rose menacingly above them, sheathed in ice.

Peter climbed the pitch leading to the Exit Cracks. Following through, Reinhold was presented with a crack that was only dimly discernible beneath the solid covering of ice. This was the point at which Hermann Bühl, Messner's old hero, had kept falling off. It was a hard pitch. At the best of times the holds were small; now the ice had to be chipped or melted from them. Each move required absolute care and deliberate execution. Peter led through and soon the two climbers were both into a rhythmic swing as pitch followed pitch and the rock gradually became less steep.

Below at the Scheidegg Hotel, Uschi would be watching through the telescope — that spyglass that had so often picked out frozen corpses on the Eigerwand. This time she would see them approaching the summit icefield and it was still not two o'clock. That would be a signal to prepare a hot bath!

Messner was just starting to congratulate himself when the sun struck the upper limits of the face. The melting process was amazingly swift. The maze of cracks and crevices turned into vertical streams and as the ice melted more stones were released. At this point they rolled and tumbled like a miniature river down towards the Spider. It was below there that the jostling stones would become lethal projectiles, whistling into space and ricocheting off the cliffs and lower icefields.

At three o'clock, Messner and Habeler sat in the sunlight on the summit of the Eiger with the Alps spreading magnificently around them. It had taken the pair exactly ten hours to do the entire face, a record time. They were back at Kleine Scheidegg after descending the easy west ridge enjoying a steaming hot bath, their clothes drying, their climbing gear strewn impotently around the hotel floor just as the four Austrians were tackling the upper Exit Cracks.

It was warm and pleasant and the tourists were milling around the balcony of the hotel, vicariously searching the huge face for signs of climbers in trouble. One of the old guides was there with his weather-beaten face and a memory packed with old dramas and old values. He looked at Messner and Habeler, shook his head in disbelief and walked away.

Chapter 12

ALPINE-STYLE IN THE HIMALAYAS

A FRAGMENT OF time flitted past as Nanga Parbat became visible in sharp detail below the wings of the droning Hercules transport plane. In one quick glance Messner could take in both the Rupal face and the Diamir face of that formidable peak; one long adventure, one brother lost, one escape — all in one glance. How would that sad achievement count in years to come? The clouds closed in and the plane flew on north-eastwards. Perhaps future generations of climbers, who would eventually have the same regard for him as he had for the Victorian pioneers, would one day be completing these massive traverses with ease; the super-fit, technically supreme mountaineers of the next centuries. Would they really be so much better, he wondered? Would materials and technology eventually allow the Himalayas to be opened up just as the Alps now were?

How too would their present exploit rank as an achievement in a hundred years' time — assuming they were successful? On the far side of the plane Peter Habeler sat wrapped in his own thoughts. The two climbers were en route from Rawalpindi to Skardu on July 12, 1975, with 200 kg. of equipment — a fraction of the weight normally carried by a Himalayan expedition. Their objective was Hidden Peak, also known as Gasherbrum I, on which they hoped to make the first Alpine-style ascent of a Himalayan summit by two men.

Previously Messner had spent several weeks at home in Villnöss orga-nising the expedition, ensuring that the red tape was neatly tied on his own mountaineering enterprise.

Hidden Peak (8,068 m.) in the Karakoram lay in the chaotic tangle of high spurs and summits that rose around the Baltoro Glacier, part of the same high pleat in the surface of the earth that had produced K2 (8,611 m., the world's second highest mountain) and Broad Peak (8,047 m.). At first it had seemed unlikely that permission to climb the mountain would be granted, so it was only at the last moment that

Messner fully believed his audacious plan would be translated into action.

His climb with Günther on Nanga Parbat had proved, despite the tragic outcome, that a lightweight ascent of an 8,000-metre peak was at least possible. The factors on that particular climb had been complicated but there was no doubt that he had been mentally and physically prepared to climb the Rupal flank and to descend it alone. Only Günther's impetuous decision to follow him had changed that. His subsequent climbs in the Himalayas had also strengthened the backbone of Messner's confidence and experience. He and Habeler were ready for a further push into the unknown; but a careful one.

So far the expedition had met with no more than the usual bureaucratic snags, but Messner had long ago learned that patience was the surest way of overcoming such problems, patience and good humour. There had also been an oppressive cloud surrounding Uschi's reaction to the trip. He had hoped to spend the summer with her up on the meadows in the Geisler Alps but that plan had been swept aside brusquely when the permission had come through and Peter had declared that he was keen to go. It was an opportunity that Messner could not miss. Everything in his climbing career had led towards it and there was no other climber he would have preferred to be with on such an attempt. His friend was superbly fit; they climbed together almost instinctively; he had an eye for the best and surest line over difficult terrain and the two men had implicit respect for one another's skill. When the chance came to work together on such a mountain as Hidden Peak, he could not ignore it and he hoped Uschi would understand that. In addition, Hans Schell, the Austrian mountaineer from Graz, had written suggesting a link-up between Messner and Habeler and his own expedition to the Baltoro area. This union, he explained, would help considerably with the financing of the expedition and would allow Schell's party too to attempt its most prized goal of Hidden Peak, though by a much easier route.

In Rawalpindi there had been no news from Uschi to relieve Messner's mind, and no sign of the Schell expedition which still only had formal permission from the authorities to attempt a lesser peak in the Baltoro region. Only Messner and Habeler had permission for Hidden Peak itself but after the Hercules touched down at Skardu, the principal town in Baltistan, it was soon clear that the others had already pressed on ahead. In one sense this was very imprudent if they still intended to attempt Hidden Peak, but at least they were making headway into the mountains. Hans Schell was obviously concentrating on reaching the mountain, leaving such issues as permissions to sort themselves out later.

After a dusty drive the two men arrived at Chalko, a village set in the baked, brown hills of Baltistan near an arm of the Braldo river. In fact the river was to prove almost as dangerous an adversary as the mountain itself. They had to cajole their porters over rope walkways across its boiling breadth and, as the gorge leading towards the Baltoro glacier grew narrower, there was an intermittent barrage of stones from the overlooking cliffs. Torrential rain made the going slower than usual and Messner started to doubt that they would ever reach the mountain in time to attempt it before the monsoon arrived. Their worryingly late arrival was accentuated by the small torrent of mountaineers who were descending from expeditions to the Baltoro area. British, Italian, Swiss and Polish climbers were all on their way home after failure or success.

Emerging from the gorge was like escaping from the frustrations and anxiety of normal life. The peaks appeared more jagged in shape as Messner led the line of porters along the narrow track. Peter had gone on ahead to advise Hans Schell not to attempt Hidden Peak but to concentrate on the mountain for which his party had permission, so Reinhold was left very much to his own thoughts which flitted about from subject to subject like some small mountain bird. Somehow he could not concentrate on the serious business that lay secreted behind an arm of the glacier, on the north-west face of Hidden Peak.

Would they really be able to make the climb in one Alpine-style rush up the 2,000 metre face, avoiding the tedious process of building up camps and stores on the mountain? Was it attempting too much to dispense with the heavy base-load of effort that was normally considered essential to put just two climbers on the summit? How much more integral it was to true achievement for two men unsupported to scale these 8,000 metre giants, the highest mountains in the world, with their cold heads thrust into the "death zone". And if that were true, he could not help thinking, how much greater the integrity if one man alone were to attempt such a climb.

Base Camp lay 72 kilometres ahead up the shattered tongue of the Baltoro Glacier. Clouds rolled heavily in: round, zinc-bottomed clouds giving the glacier and its long badger-stripes of debris a dull grey monotony and spilling cold puddles of mist over the ice. The glacier snout was an ice cliff, a wall of untidy blocks and stones up which the porters clambered forlornly with bare feet. Messner climbed ahead on the ridge formed by a length of moraine, and marked out the safe route for the men and their loads. This gave him time to marvel at the shifts in colour and texture caused by the changes of light as the clouds rolled by and the

Manaslu: the view from Base Camp

Above and left:
Climbing on Manaslu

Franz Jaeger   Andi Schlick

Aconcagua: Dr Oswald Ölz

The route up Aconcagua

Strong wind on Makalu

Rawalpindi with Peter Habeler en route to Hidden Peak, 1975

Habeler and seracs on Hidden Peak

With Uschi and
the dogs just
after divorce,
1977

sun moved to a new angle. Some of the peaks — Trango Towers, Little Cathedral Peak and the Biafo Tower — he recognised from photographs: vast rock forms rising from the frozen waves of the glacier, their faces aged with thin crow's feet of snow. But their wildness finally quelled all concern, even about Uschi, and Messner concentrated on shepherding the porters up to the head of the Baltoro Glacier, then along the lateral spur of the Abruzzi Glacier to the start of the climb.

Hans Schell had set his base camp close in to the mountain and was coolly preparing to attempt the IHE spur, first climbed in 1958 by the Americans and which, Hans argued, would not in any way detract from Messner and Habeler's achievement on the opposite side of the mountain. He was keen to add an 8,000 metre peak to a lifetime's list of fine climbing achievements.

Reinhold and his partner weighed their reaction. What would the mountaineering historians say? Would they wag their sage heads and deny their own achievement, insisting it was hardly a two-man success when there was a full-scale expedition just round the corner? But what did this matter so long as Messner and Habeler themselves felt sure of the integrity of their climb? Let the heads wag. Reinhold grinned at Hans Schell and shook his hand. The stocky Austrian grinned back with relief. The climbing permit would be shared, with goodwill.

The two expeditions went their separate ways. Reinhold and Peter headed up into the Gasherbrum Valley and took a closer look at the north-west face of Hidden Peak. They bivouacked on the glacier and watched the sunset send low shafts of light directly across the mountain, enabling them to pick out the deep creases where ice had built up thickly into large seracs. There was a choice of two routes but closer inspection from the Gasherbrum Col, which they reached the following morning, showed that the right-hand possibility was so threatened by the seracs that it was probably too dangerous. The other line looked as though it might be menaced by stonefalls in its lower half. It cut directly up an icy bowl to the left-hand ridge which it then followed to the summit. They agreed that this would be the most logical route to try, and determined to go ahead in the next spell of good weather.

Dawn and consciousness melted their way through a veil of vivid dreams. The dreams dissolved and re-formed as grey, gravel-stained ice, sending up a cold reflection of reality which greeted them as they emerged from the tent. With the first light, Peter set out thoughtfully towards the face, his body already moving with swift, neat assurance. This was it then. This was the moment, but so like the beginning of any other mountain day: sleepiness and the frosty nip on the inside of the nostrils, turning breath to steam; uneven ground crunching beneath his boots; the heavy drag of a rucksack across his shoulders and a million deliberate paces lined up ahead, waiting to be taken.

Reinhold caught up with him and moved into the lead. The sky was still bright with stars which the rising sun had not yet erased. The air was still, the mountain quiet and the silence infected them both with a feeling of delighted anticipation. The ground steepened and he felt that exhilarating sense of challenge which usually came when a mountainside tilted under his feet and dared him not to fall off. From now on, it seemed to say, he would have to struggle to make headway: from that point he would be under threat.

The two men strapped on crampons and neutralised the steepness of the glacier. The sun slid a wedge of brightness down the opposite cliffs but still left Hidden Peak a chill grey. A broad crevasse splitting the glacier appeared in front of them and the two climbers halted. They shared out the pitons and ice screws, checked their climbing harnesses and a short length of rope, which they carried to safeguard themselves across crevasses, and moved across the gap.

Shortly after 7 a.m. the sunlight triggered the first avalanches and they heard them thundering down the sunny side of the mountain. They set up their first bivouac at 5,900 metres at the foot of the actual face, away from the path of any lethal debris. By now the sun was beating down fiercely, expanding the already thin air and making the heat stifling. Peter had a bad headache and lay down in the tent. Messner lay in the bivouac beside him to get some rest before the real climbing began.

The next day was clear and fine. Once more there was that superb flood of sunlight down the opposite peaks and a matching surge of confidence in themselves. The snow was soft on the surface, then there was a compacted layer into which their front crampon points sank securely. They took turns to lead, the first man both breaking trail and determining the route, the second securing a degree of relaxation from the effort of climbing.

After each dozen steps they rested, cutting a small platform in the ice to relieve the tension on leg muscles, which was intensified by the thick, high altitude boots. Peter climbed with a steady rhythm and style that Reinhold could not help but admire. It was curious, he reflected, that they had not climbed together more often. Reinhold had done probably fewer than a dozen routes with Peter — but what routes! The explanation perhaps was that they were quite different temperamentally:

Messner self-contained and Habeler more genial and extrovert. Away from the ultimate stress of a hard and committing climb, they had rather less in common — and both men had separate circles of friends.

Reinhold observed the soles of his companion's cramponed boots, kicking steadily into the slope above his head. The sun was now catching the face they were on and loosening stones that had been frozen into the ice. The barrage began slowly but built up to an unremitting bombardment.

Below them the impression of a vast white vacuum was steadily growing. Above them the wall rose into space for 2,000 metres. Messner could see the sharp outline of a row of overhangs which stretched across their path. They knew already from their reconnaissance that their next bivouac lay beyond this barrier.

Despite the steepness and exposed nature of the climb the two men moved together. It reflected their confidence in one another and the degree to which they were committed to completing the route as swiftly as possible. Soon they reached the tier of overhangs which turned out to be a rock step projecting from the face. Reinhold approached the first steep pitch and took his gloves off, the better to grip the rock, though he felt the sensation drain from his fingers. Watched closely by Peter he moved out gingerly using pressure holds and hand jams. Peter soon followed, teeth chattering with cold and the effect of the thin air which forced him to breathe convulsively.

In *The Challenge** Messner was later to recall this section of the climb most vividly:

"Leaning my head right back, I gazed upwards; the sky was matt white with a blue background. Out on the horizon where it met the snowy crests, the blue was even mistier. The west-facing snow slopes sparkled brilliantly. The view towards the sun was unbearable. Below us, the valleys were visible in a bluish haze, blue with a touch of violet in it, an almost magical effect. Here and there the mist appeared to be bubbling, as if the earth below was boiling. As I hung, poised between heaven and earth, it seemed that there were unfathomable depths below, unfathomable heights above. We were 1,200 metres from the summit, more than 2,000 metres from the valley bottom. My thoughts swam like the blue haze beneath me — another 200 metres and we should be safe.

"The gully narrowed into a chimney. With legs spread wide, I straddled up the crack. The rock was sounder here. I didn't care to think whether or not I could save myself if I were to slip. So I pressed more firmly

* *The Challenge* by Reinhold Messner, Kaye and Ward Ltd., 1977

with my hands against the parallel sides of the chimney. If I were to slip only a short distance, I must surely take Peter with me. He could never hold me if I fell. The chimney now narrowed, which was a piece of luck; it was now easier to wedge ourselves into it.

"I continued up another gully until I came to a ridge on my left, and climbing onto this, I reached the shoulder between the North and North-west faces. Here I rested. A steep wall now reared above me, rocky in places, all its hollows filled with packed snow. It looked as if it could avalanche at any minute. I was undecided whether or not to go on, and consoled myself that once over this steep rise, we should find our next bivouac spot."

Peter then took over the lead, the concentration involved in making hard, exposed climbing moves transcending the weakening effects of the thin air and intense cold. The snow was crumbly and in order to dispose his weight over as wide an area as possible he thrust in his ice-axe high above his head and pulled on it, moving his body steadily higher up the face and shaking with the effort. Watching him and waiting to follow, Messner felt his own legs begin to shake, not from fear but from the effort of holding himself there, tacked tenuously to the mountainside by only the front points of his crampons.

The two men emerged from the huge snow bowl on to the ridge and saw an ideal bivouac site, a hollow filled with ice and rocks which after ten hours on that steep face looked as inviting as an interior-sprung mattress. They had climbed over 1,200 metres that day and felt very satisfied. Peter grinned as he stretched out luxuriantly in the shelter of the bivouac. Messner rested his head on his rucksack and felt the enormous tension drain from his body.

"What do you think?" Peter asked, cheerfully.

"I reckon the worst is over now, just that last 1,000 metres to the top, but the ground is much less steep."

"What about going down? We can't reverse those rocks."

"Perhaps there will be a crack that we can descend; I don't know."

"We should have brought a full-length rope," Peter murmured.

Peter had climbed superbly that day, moving without hesitation, absolutely confident. But now again he had begun to show the signs of illness that always attacked him when he reached a higher level of altitude — the blinding headache that always made him feel so wretched.

Peter swallowed a couple of tablets washed down with lukewarm tea and waited for the pain to subside. Outside, the night was clear and star-studded and hoar frost gathered thickly on the tent walls. The air was exceptionally still. They had a meal, then settled down in their sleeping bags, trying to forget that only one piton and a few loose rocks held their little shelter to the mountainside.

At seven o'clock they were awake again, well rested. Peter felt much better and in eager anticipation of the climb extricated his boots from the sleeping bag where he had been keeping them warm. They emptied their rucksacks of everything not essential to the day's climb and set out heading for a hollow in the summit area that looked from the valley like a recumbent sickle. They made good if slow progress; up through the sickle they went, and on above the faint veil of cloud that misted the lower reaches of Hidden Peak. With each step more summits came into view on a vast, curving horizon serrated with mountain tops. K2 appeared among them, a fine pyramid, head and shoulders higher than its neighbours.

The two climbers moved on with their leaden rhythm, changing places every 60 metres or so, the leader breaking the trail and stirring up a fine cloud of powder snow, the second following like a robot. Reinhold stopped, suddenly aware that all sensation had departed from his right foot. He called to Peter to halt and carefully peeled the layers of protection from his foot until he could massage some circulation back into the stumps of his amputated toes.

There was no wind; the air was perfectly calm. Suddenly the slope eased and they were on the summit surrounded by a silent monochrome world of ice and rock and the blue-black vault of the sky with the Abruzzi Glacier appearing on the western side of the mountain.

There was a quiet sense of elation and a feeling of standing at the threshold of infinity until the ordinary imperatives prodded them into action again. They retreated along their tracks in the hard snow back to the bivouac and by late afternoon were cooking a meal and melting snow. Soon after that they crawled into their sleeping bags. Reinhold counted not sheep but steps, slow ponderous steps that left hollows in an endless white slope.

The next thing he was aware of was a cold flurry of spindrift being blown into his face. He pulled the down-filled hood over his head and struggled to regain the deep sleep, but the insistent skeins of snow refused to let him do so. He opened his eyes and saw that the end of the bivouac tent was torn. Then he became aware of the wind. It was howling and tearing at the tent fabric. There was no need to shake Peter awake. Alarm, like an electric shock, brought both men out of the tent into the full blast of the storm. Without them in it, the tent immediately began to tear itself to shreds. They packed only essentials and immediately turned towards the descent route, climbing down over the comfortable edge and on to the steep inner face of the bowl. After the first few feet the wind diminished slightly and they were protected by the bulk of the mountain.

As Peter moved downwards below him, Reinhold saw him inch towards the start of a chimney which could possibly be an alternative to the fiercely exposed face. Pitch by pitch they went down the mountain, meeting succeeding bands of crumbling snow and steel-hard ice. A rope, he reflected, would have been of little use. There were not enough reliable belays and they were not carrying a sufficient number and variety of pegs. A rope would simply have meant the danger of both men falling instead of one.

Messner's diary recorded 600 metres descent in four hours, which took them half way to the foot of the slope. By now they were both gasping with fatigue and Peter's features looked to have aged: the skin was wrinkled and his eyes dark with exhaustion.

"This goes on for ever more," Peter said wearily, as Reinhold halted to allow him to move through and take the lead. He moved down, paused and slipped off his rucksack, letting it fall down the face. They watched it accelerate terribly against the rocks and ice and disappear from view into the Gasherbrum valley. Peter felt mightily relieved of the heavy weight and looked up to Reinhold who also slipped off his sack and dropped it into the void.

The next stretch of time seemed endless, focused only on the ice wall six inches in front of their faces. Messner climbed like an automaton, never shifting more than one point of contact at a time; his top security the tip of his axe and an ice piton, his feet pinned to the wall by the points of his crampons. His legs were now beyond the pain of stress, his tongue was swollen and throat felt parched. It was not until the angle finally eased that they knew they were safe. Beyond that immediate realisation Messner was already wrestling with the implications of their climb. After one month of acclimatising, two men unaided had climbed a hard 8,000 metre peak and had taken only five days. It later proved they had reached the summit one day ahead of the Austrians even though the larger expedition had started out two weeks ahead of them and its members had used oxygen and fixed their route with ropes.

Later, too, Messner reflected on the significance of the success. Had they merely climbed a mountain in a slightly different way from the general run of expeditions? Or had they achieved more than that? A group of Polish climbers they had met near their base camp had congratulated them on finding a new dimension for the sport. Two men without oxygen and without rope had completed this unremitting climb. But

Messner's thoughts went beyond that. Peter had been a great assurance; a palpable anchor, almost as though there had been a rope between them. But never had either of them had to rely totally on the other. What two men could do without help surely one man could do alone. Had they not proved, therefore, that an 8,000 metre summit was possible alone?

Chapter 13

MOUNTAINS AND MARRIAGE DO NOT MIX

WHAT BEGAN AS a hobby had become a serious full-time profession. Public interest in Messner centred on how far his latest exploits set new standards of daring. The further he succeeded and the more often he returned from such exploits, the keener public interest became in him. But the balance was critical between measuring what he thought possible against what he recognised as a growing appetite for vicarious adventure among the public. It was a forbidding kind of professionalism but it was now too late to change; or if not too late he was too fascinated with discovering where his own limits lay to seek any other way of life. The rationalisation was simple enough. Two thousand Alpine routes and now some of the hardest, highest mountains in the world. He was clearly not the type to whom "unlucky" things happened; not at least in the mountains. His judgement was proven. On Lhotse and Makalu he had turned back, recognising that the balance of good sense was against going on.

But who was dictating the pace? Messner himself, the ego of a man who had achieved so much and sought to achieve so much more? Was it the mountains themselves which formed the challenge, or was it the public, whose interest provided the finance for him to keep returning to fresh attempts and who were as keen as Messner himself to see the next threshold yield? After all, Messner was not alone in the field of climbing exploration. The standards were rising rapidly in both the Alps and the Himalayas and the competition to achieve "firsts" was intense. The Japanese and British mountaineers were showing great determination in the Himalayas in attacking the remaining goals. It would be extremely difficult for one man to stay ahead of the field, to keep selecting targets which were both startling and attainable and, above all, to keep coming back.

Uschi never doubted that Reinhold would always return. Her own life had become inextricably linked with mountaineering and with helping to make sure that his crowded schedule went smoothly, with lecture tours, interviews, negotiations, television appearances and publishing all taking up more time than was ever available between expeditions.

They had lived together for five years before Uschi began to feel the strain; not of the practical problems of being wife, secretary, agent and public relations officer to Messner, but of living continually in his shadow. A sense that her own personality, her own life and ambitions were being suffocated became very strong. She buried her feelings but the worm of discontent was always there, eating away all the more voraciously as Reinhold's plans grew more and more ambitious. He was achieving his purpose, his sense of fulfilment, but she had given up the life of a Baroness for the uncertainty of living with a professional adventurer. She had seen remote corners of the world, lived with strange and primitive communities and felt the excitement of attempting what had never been attempted, but always in the shadow of this determined man. She could love and admire him but equally feel infuriated by him. It was like living permanently in the vortex of a whirlwind.

Reinhold recognised the change in Uschi and was dismayed by it. He had grown to rely heavily on her both as an organiser of his increasingly complicated life and as a companion. What he experienced was enriched by sharing it with her. He had never for an instant doubted that if there was some curious alchemy in life that matched one person to another, then he and Uschi were the halves of that matching formula. It was a curious and a subtle mixture of qualities and it was particularly her ironic sense of humour that he needed. She showed no hint of hero worship, no sense of awe at his achievements. Thank heavens for that. Just a steady good nature and a withering scorn for anyone who attempted to dress up Messner's feats in pseudo-psychology.

By this stage journalists and doctors were pursuing their own professional sport by dissecting the mountaineer's motives and character. Some declared that he had an oedipal complex, that he was busily burying homosexual desire beneath the bravado of danger, that he was fundamentally lunatic.

"The one thing they seem to fail to understand," Uschi told him one day, "is that you like climbing mountains, that you are rather good at climbing mountains and that you prefer to do what you like doing. That, of course, is far too simple for these people."

Early in 1977 Messner heard that the Nepalese government had granted him permission to attempt another 8,000 metre peak, this time the south face of Dhaulagiri. Uschi was to go with him to Nepal and lead a trekking party while he and a small group of climbers attempted the forbidding face.

The press, after a brief look, found Dhaulagiri an easy peak to sensationalise. One magazine reported that since 1969 it had killed twelve mountaineers. Five Sherpas had suffocated in avalanches, struck down by falling blocks of ice or swallowed up in glacier crevasses. In relation to the small number of people who had attempted the mountain, the death rate was quite unequalled. The south face was regarded by experts as "terrible" because of its steepness and proneness to avalanches. It was, said one, murderously open to stonefall and impossible to climb at the time of year when Messner intended to make his attempt.

The expedition was indeed to prove one of the most unhappy for Messner, partly because of the mountain's dangers but also for other reasons. As they arrived at Munich airport to catch the plane for Nepal, an envelope was handed to Uschi. It was from her former husband Max von Kienlin. Inside was a note saying that one of their daughters had been badly scalded at home in an accident. He enclosed a photograph of the girl, showing scald marks on her face. On the way out to Nepal, Uschi was deeply concerned, torn by guilt over her children. They were being well looked after, obviously, and all children had accidents at some stage. If she had been there, she argued with herself, it would not have prevented the accident. Even so, the letter and the photograph tipped the balance in her mind. Surely she was being grossly selfish in seeking only her own self-realisation at the expense of the children? She could not expect Reinhold to help. They were not his children; they had nothing at all to do with him. The decisions had been all her own; she must act.

Messner and the others set out towards Dhaulagiri. Uschi departed with her group, feeling deeply unhappy. Soon the two parties were divided by the Gandaki Gorge, said to be the deepest defile in the world which Uschi, at that moment, felt to be significant. She wanted desperately to see her children and that ache added to the discontent she now keenly felt in her life with Reinhold. She had given up the positive but routine life of a mother to live as an adventurer in the shadow of this powerful man who overwhelmed her and inadvertently crushed her own personality. She could no longer tolerate being a kind of matrimonial dockyard to which Messner could return occasionally for shelter and repairs.

Uschi therefore determined to leave, to break off the marriage if that was necessary, and start life again alone. She returned to Germany while Messner was still battling with Dhaulagiri, and finding it quite as dangerous as the pessimists had said it would be. After the climbers had watched their route being pounded by a series of spectacular avalanches they waited without reward for conditions to improve. Eventually, the attempt was abandoned.

By this time Messner was anxious about Uschi and about their future. There was no letter, no message from her. The expedition had been a failure but he had not in any case been able to concentrate single-mindedly on the climbing. In the background he had been aware of his wife's unhappiness. There were few people in the world he had ever felt really close to, no one he had ever committed himself to unselfishly except Uschi. He had never doubted or regretted their decision to get married in spite of the chaos that this caused to other lives. The powerful attraction between them, the qualities that made Uschi different from any other woman he had met, had never weakened for Reinhold. He had deliberately made Uschi important to him and was quite unable to reverse that decision, to treat their relationship as an unsuccessful ascent, shrug his shoulders and philosophically walk away. That was impossible, and when he returned to Villnöss and found the house empty, Reinhold was filled with the most overwhelming black despair he had known.

Their home at St. Magdalena seemed doubly empty: no one was there waiting and it seemed certain no one would come. There was no message from Uschi and he could not contact her by telephone. But, he asked himself, how could he honestly feel even surprised that she should decide to leave? There had been so many warnings. Once she had asked him directly: "If you had to choose between the mountains and me, which would it be?" and he had not replied. He had looked glumly resentful at the question, fumbled for words or changed the subject; anything rather than face such a stark option.

Uschi was right and so, without admitting it, was he. He was torn by two irreconcilable desires. When he was away climbing in the Himalayas he would always write home tenderly and wish strongly for them to be together. Yet when he was home his mind would quickly turn to the next adventure, his thoughts focus somewhere beyond Villnöss, on some new goal which Uschi could not totally be part of. He had much of the glamour, all the adulation; she was left with reflected fame and a lot of hard work helping to organise the adventures.

Clearly the break-up of her earlier marriage and the separation from her children had wounded Uschi. There had been a private burden of grief and Reinhold could have helped simply by being there. Leaving Uschi alone only allowed the grief to grow. There had been a choice. When the opportunities came he could have said "No", or delayed his plans in order to reassure Uschi and devote more time to her.

Many climbers and explorers must have reached this same impasse in their relationships with their families. It was the positive and self-contained nature of the man that had made Reinhold attractive to Uschi. He commanded respect; a man, by his very nature, apart from men. Yet that nature isolated him and set a strict order to his priorities. Human relations would always take second place even though he loved Uschi more than any other human being. Now, at the crunch, he was unable to change that immutable order of priorities.

Perhaps he was too deeply committed to the harsh regime of extreme climbing, of setting his life in the scales against some barely feasible ambition. There were many questions which the emptiness of St. Magdalena now made irrelevant because the chance to answer them was lost. He felt a numbing certainty that Uschi would not return. They had married in the summer of 1972. They were divorced in 1977.

His reaction to the break-up was more severe than he had expected. Always he had returned to Uschi's cheerful calm after the risk and action of an expedition. Now there was an emptiness more terrible than he could admit. He tried to swamp himself in new plans for fresh expeditions but nothing would fall into place. Immediately after the abortive attempt on Dhaulagiri he had gone with one of his younger brothers, Hans Jorg, to Nanga Parbat. They did not even reach the foot of the Diamir face. For Reinhold the powerful wish to return home and the despair over Uschi had been overwhelming.

For months he could not adjust to being alone and it was not until the possibility of an attempt on Everest began to form that the desperate feeling of isolation began to subside. With Peter Habeler and many of his old climbing companions, he started to feel the old challenging spirit returning. To train and to become better acclimatised he went out to Kilimanjaro in Africa and completed one classic and one extremely hard new route on Breach Wall.

He returned to Europe in the spring of 1978. The Austrian expedition was preparing to set out for Everest and he threw himself completely into this new enterprise, convincing himself that it was feasible and relishing the chance to make such a frontier-breaking climb. The loss of Uschi in a way gave him something to fight free of. It was a numbing feeling that caused him to make a total commitment to climbing Everest. For Peter, who had a wife and a young son, that commitment was perhaps harder to make, but for Reinhold the idea of laying his life on the line in an ultimate gamble was a therapeutic action, something positive after so many months of despair.

Chapter 14

RETURN ALONE TO NANGA PARBAT

IMMEDIATELY AFTER THE success on Everest Reinhold finalised his plans for a solo attempt on Nanga Parbat. In the summer of 1978 he felt that he was in perfect shape for the attempt: fit, rested and well acclimatised. Most important, Everest had proved to him that a solo climb of an 8,000 metre peak was possible.

He would also, he thought, be happy to escape the avalanche of public interest and speculation that had greeted him after the Everest climb. The reception back in Italy and Germany had been quite fantastic, far greater than he had ever imagined. As ever, there were the doubters. In Nepal some leading Sherpas had suggested that he and Peter could not have done what they claimed, that they had really had small phials of oxygen hidden in their jackets to sniff on the way up! Others blandly said there was nothing unusual in going to high altitude without oxygen. Tensing Norgay pointed out that he had been to the south summit of Everest a couple of times without oxygen.

In Europe there were no doubters but a hail of publicity: television and newspapermen, crowded lectures and a book to complete. The feat even dragged him momentarily into the political arena. A leading politician in South Tyrol had told an audience of 3,000 in Bolzano: ''Here is Reinhold Messner, our great mountaineer who has done this incredible thing for South Tyrol.'' Messner was quick to his feet to point out that was wrong. He did not believe in such narrow nationalism. ''I did it only for me,'' he told the audience.

There were whistle-stop tours, appearances on television where Messner became something of a guru on philosophy, religion, politics — any subject including, occasionally, mountains.

There had been no time to worry about his broken relationship with Uschi. The whirl of activity was the best balm to a troubled spirit. Now he was back in the Himalayas with permission to make a solo attempt on Nanga Parbat, arriving like a tourist at the foot of the mountain with his tent and rucksack and walking straight up it. He had never been better prepared for such a climb either physically or mentally. Everest had not only toughened him and given him a high degree of acclimatisation but it had removed any doubts in his mind, any lurking uncertainty that he might not be able to stand up to the pressures of such a high altitude solo climb. Was he setting himself more and more unrealistic goals? He thought not. Everest was perhaps technically easier than Nanga Parbat but it was almost three thousand feet higher. He knew this face both from his descent with Günther and his attempt in 1973 when he had reached over 6,000 metres. There were seracs and rocks and the possibility of avalanches; an avalanche had killed Günther. But if it was all weighed in the balance there was a chance, though by no means a certainty, that he could climb Nanga Parbat alone. He wanted to find out as a personal experiment, to discover his own limits, to innovate and to be the first in a world where "firsts" were hard to come by.

His experience now was so phenomenal that he could reasonably attempt such a climb which for an average climber would be either impossible or suicidal. He felt such attempts were within the scope of his ability. He believed that very positively. His proven endurance, speed and control made it easier for him to convince himself. This meant being hard, sometimes ruthlessly positive. Sensitive folk listened to him and thought that he was unfeeling. They misunderstood. The price for such detachment and self-containment was the kind of relationship that relied on formal niceties. For Messner life was too vital, too great and too short for any sort of posturing. It was easier now to say: "Accept me as I am or go away."

The accusations of his having caused Günther's death, the sniping from folk who were basically envious of his prowess, all of which had stung bitterly at the time, were now buried beneath a thick skin of achievement. Being among mountains and climbing them made the carping seem irrelevant and left him untouched. Climbing was, to him, as much a mental exercise as physical movement over difficult rock and ice. What he could achieve was "all in the mind". He had only to produce fragments of evidence to convince himself that other achievements were perfectly possible, and his body was prepared for yet more challenges. He was completely aware of the objective dangers and skilful at anticipating them. Mountains remained as deadly for him as for anyone else except that through experience he had moved the odds against having an accident rather more in his favour. He had not eliminated them altogether.

In July 1978, little more than two months after reaching the summit of Everest with Peter Habeler, Messner was camped in the Diamir valley beneath the western flank of Nanga Parbat. There were three in the party: Reinhold, Dr Ursula Grether and Mohammed Tahir (known as Terry), the liaison officer. Tall, blond and cool-mannered, Ursula came from Heidelberg and Reinhold had met her when she turned up at Everest base camp. She had been a great help then, treating casualties and helping in an operation on one of the Sherpas, and Messner had decided to invite her back to the Himalayas.

Their base camp was in an idyllic place, set beneath the flank of the mountain and overlooking a broad sweep of lesser ridges and heavily vegetated countryside, with the bright ribbon of a river running through it. The deep cut of the Indus valley was just visible in the furthest distance.

The walk-in had been relaxing after the bustle of Germany in the wake of the Everest climb; day after day of quiet progress through this superb countryside; ample time to think and to plan and no feeling of fear or impending danger. How different from his last attempt alone on Nanga Parbat when he had felt so wretched and uncertain. Here he was again, the same person with the same objective but an entirely different attitude.

When Base Camp was established and the equipment sorted out, Messner lay listening to the sounds of the mountain in the darkness outside the tent; the rustling of the stream that meandered down from the ice, the slight rattle of the wind on the canvas, the hollow acoustics that the presence of a big mountain sometimes gives.

The day dawned fair. Ursula and Terry helped with the small amount of packing that was required as the pale light caught the snowfields of the mountain and then spread to the grey, towering buttresses of rock. Immediately around the camp the countryside had the look of an Alpine meadow. The grass had a sweet, luxuriant smell, the sun was warm and the view superb. The signs among the glaciers and summit ridges were good today. They had noted that weather in the region followed an almost predictable pattern. A good spell seemed about to begin so the time had come to start out.

He checked the equipment: a few slings, an ice screw and a solitary piton, his bivouac tent with the flexible fibreglass hoops. He checked the metal segments of his crampons minutely, his gas stove and supplies of food: packet soups and lightweight fare containing a lot of energy. The whole load weighed about 22 kilos, enough to survive for a week or more in an ultimately hostile environment. His clothing was the same as for Everest: silk underwear, a windproof one-piece climbing suit and down outer clothing. Finally, he packed spare goggles and mitts and his ice axe with the camera attachment for auto-photography. Reinhold had had a screw fitting fixed to the axe, so that he could jam the axe into the snow and set the automatic mechanism, giving himself time to scramble into the picture.

At 5 a.m. on August 6 Messner stepped steadily through the glacier debris above the camp. Higher up, a narrow bridge separated the main thrust of ice from the Diamir face and the Mazeno face, an unclimbed 3,500 metre rock and ice wall. Ahead was the first technical difficulty, a 20 metre ice wall on the edge of the gully down which the main avalanches flowed. Further up there was an ice bulge overhanging in places and blocking the way. These obstacles were hard to pick out through a telescope. It was only when a climber stood beneath them that such Gordian knots could be examined and perhaps untied.

He had been climbing for four hours when the sun flooded on to the face and there was the rattle of stones loosened by its heat. The fortress wall grew higher still over to the right and the way above was no longer clear. He tried to remember details of the face at this point from the flattened perspective of base camp.

"Over to the left." The voice was clear and English.

"Are you sure?" Messner replied. He was startled. He was after all alone. He moved to the left and saw a line of weakness emerging. Whoever it was was right: a steep chimney which he straddled with a foot on each wall, body held in balance by the hands. Suddenly the obstacle was no longer an obstacle.

There was no time now to reflect about fears or presentiments of falling bodies or even to notice that they had all vanished. There was no room for them. Everything was in brittle focus; he moved like a ruthless automaton highly charged with energy. From the chill shadow of the chimney the light was warm again, sunlight flooding over the Diamir face and Messner's whole concentration directed to the intricate upward route. Existence was suddenly blinkered, excluding everything except the next hold or the next general line, a secure and committed world.

The base camp tents were small flecks of colour in a huge landscape. He was looking for signs of life there when he became aware of a figure close at hand but just out of his field of vision. He sensed that his father was there moving ahead, steadily leading the way, unseen like the owner of the English voice, but there nevertheless. Messner followed. A long easy-angled ice-slope slipped by beneath the points of his crampons in a steady rhythm. Fragments of childhood memories went through his mind: the early climbs with his father; the Dolomites where the rock was steep and warm and familiar; the wall outside their home in St. Peter; the old saw mill with its pungent smell of damp wood. Lots of memories, many climbs. The closeness of his family, the decision, if there ever had been anything so firm and positive as a decision, to devote his life to climbing. The enjoyment he had from trying to express in words what he felt about climbing, although this could be frustrating because such sensation, the freedom, the self-knowledge and the satisfaction were hardly containable in anything so bald as a sentence. It was an instinct, deeply rooted and profound to him. Put into words it could sound so pontifical, so egocentric.

Messner paused, straightened his shoulders beneath the heavy rucksack. The mountain had already changed under this steady, ceaseless slog. Nanga Parbat felt bigger, more immediate. The surrounding peaks were diminishing. He checked the reading on his altimeter. This instrument had recorded some formidable heights and had become rather mountainworn. The inscription on the back read: "To the Conqueror of Eight-Thousanders from his Friends in the CAI Belledo Section — 29.10.74''. A little further on, in the shelter of an ice bulge and clear of any falling debris, he put up his bivouac tent and immediately began melting snow for a drink. As always in this airless, elemental place it was essential to drink as much water as he could force down to prevent dehydration. He had covered a good distance and noted in his diary: "Comfortable night, slept deeply, no dreams.''

Again next day he made an early start before dawn and moved up into the danger zone of the Diamir face. The huge wall of Mazeno still towered over him, reminding him of the long distance still to go. At such close quarters it was difficult to orientate himself. He could pick out the Mummery Rib and further over the huge barrier of seracs 200 metres high and curving round, blockading the upper reaches of the face.

So far, progress had been excellent: at least 500 metres of height gained per hour and no ill effects felt from the altitude. The summit still appeared endlessly distant but there was a thrilling sense of loneliness and self-sufficiency — none of fear. When he reached the 6,200-metre level, the danger from collapsing seracs was past.

Before the sun started to loosen everything he decided to make his second bivouac, tucked beneath a substantial-looking serac. He felt strong and fit and untired by his swift climb. It was going well. He was confident. He wondered whether Ursula could pick him out through the telescope, a small black dot against the gigantic chaos of the face.

The altimeter read over 6,500 metres but he felt no effect from the altitude. The conditions up here were settled and there were no serious signs that the weather was likely to break. He cut out a place beneath the serac for his tent and settled in, watching through the door the movement in the air below him where vaporous mist was swirling around and consolidating into dense banks of cloud. He melted more snow and settled down with his thoughts. The bivouac was as safe as anywhere on this unstable mountain, and snug, with his ground mat and sleeping bag unrolled and the stove hissing away.

As he rested, the sense of someone standing close by remained, a strong physical presence intangible yet extremely real and not at all threatening. Quite the opposite. Messner could not rationalise this feeling nor accept its connection with his remoteness or the thinness of the air. It was simply there, real as a companion. He had the feeling of being a kind of landbound Joshua Slocum, the first man to sail alone around the world.

The bag in the roof of the tent was packed with snow which dripped constantly into a beaker. And in the early hours of the morning Messner felt nausea creeping on him. He lay there in his tent quietly vomiting. Then came the earthquake.

It happened without warning in the icy stillness of early light on August 8. Not altogether without warning: when Messner woke up at 5 a.m., his altimeter had been reading 50 metres higher than the previous night — a sign that a huge pressure front was passing and not that he had drifted higher up the mountain. The first crash came shortly after 8 a.m. with a terrible suddenness. The battering din shook the tent and brought Messner out of his sleeping bag to tear at the entrance of the bivouac tent. The roaring continued until it reached a violent crescendo. He was fearful that the serac immediately above him would join this sudden wild eruption of the mountainside. Outside, to the left, ice avalanches roared down, sucking in the air and creating an instant blizzard. Even more terrible, the ice cliff beneath which he had been climbing was collapsing in huge blocks. The whole mountain was alive and shaking — Messner assumed at first that it was an avalanche but it was worse than any that he had ever been near before. A tidal wave of ice and snow swept from the cliff in a solid Niagara and fanned out across the face, a long grey tongue licking with deadly menace towards Base Camp.

Messner's heart was pounding with shock. He looked down at the route he had climbed the previous day. It had been wiped out by the apocalyptic rush of the avalanche. Before it reached the end of the glacier the explosion of snow halted but the whole basin area of the Diamir face looked as if it had been destroyed by artillery bombardment. Millions of tons of mountainside had crashed into it. He realised that he was safe, but if he had not climbed with such speed yesterday, or if he had been in a conventional expedition making its way ponderously up the face. . . .

He stopped speculating, and with deliberate calmness and thoroughness folded up the small tent and packed it into his rucksack with his food and equipment. The upper section of the mountain had not been so scoured by the avalanches as the lower. Never had he seen such devastation or heard such a fearful din, the terrible crack of earth fracturing and being unleashed with totally destructive force.

He closed his mind to what might have happened — or tried to. His sickness had gone, driven away perhaps by a massive rush of adrenalin.

A cold wind moaned over the mountainside and Messner felt chilled. He forced himself to start climbing although his limbs were stiff and his body could not pick up the steady rhythm he had achieved so easily the day before. The snow surface felt brittle and insecure. His rucksack was heavy. He had abandoned any idea of leaving a small cache of food and equipment at the bivouac site for the descent. That part of the Diamir face was now too torn and unstable. He would have to find another way down.

He climbed on, moving slowly through the difficult snow towards a point where a serac, split as if by a blow from a gigantic axe, offered an escape on to the shallower-angled ground leading towards the summit area. The going was painfully slow. Each hour he gained only a fraction of the altitude he had managed the previous day, and the mountain now had an ugly look.

Avalanches continued to grumble down the Diamir flank, less spectacular than the earlier explosion but still dangerous. A thin veil of cirrus cloud was drawing in from the west and gathering around the summit, a bad sign, he thought, but then this had been an exceptionally bad day. Avalanches at this hour were very unusual and such a fierce barrage was quite unheard of. What the hell was happening? He rightly concluded that Nanga Parbat had been struck by an earthquake.

He was now toiling on to the highest part of the Diamir flank. The Mazeno wall was below him and other mountain ranges opened up to the west. The scene was exhilarating and sent a charge of strength through him. He climbed more positively. "No point in worrying about those avalanches," he said aloud, "or which way down to go. I am still alive, unscathed and feeling okay. No problems; well, not so many problems."

This was addressed to his shadowy companion who still lurked in the corner of his vision. The sun broke through the clouds in mid-morning as he trudged through the 7,000 metre level towards the huge summit block.

The altitude was now making itself felt again. Every few steps he was forced to stop and control his breathing and the pounding of his heart. He could feel the blood banging through his temples. The sun made the snow surface softer and he began to look around in vain for another safe bivouac site. There was only snow, deep unpleasant sun-softened snow. "Rest; rest in the snow, sleep." No, don't be an idiot, you must make a proper bivouac. You must climb on. "No, rest; rest here." The voice was seductive. He forced himself to his feet again and scraped out the heavy snow that had balled up solidly between his crampon points.

His breath rasped harshly. His throat felt brittly parched and beyond the deep tiredness which reached to the core of his body, Messner began to feel alone; he had a terrible and sharp awareness that there was no one who could help him if he failed.

It took him over half an hour to erect the tent, fill the snow sack and climb into the small shelter. But being inside improved his spirits. It cut out the immediate prospect of a steep, desolate mountainside and blurred the fact that he was the only person on it. Water began dripping from the sack of snow. His body felt rested and the first drink acted like rain on a desert. He had ceased to worry about what was happening outside the tent, even though there was an ocean of solid cloud billowing up immediately below him and blocking off the base of the mountain. He felt a pang of concern for Ursula and Terry at Base Camp. It was probably dreadful down there and they would be full of anxiety about where he was and what conditions were like for him. There was no way he could let them know that all was well.

He warmed some soup and made another drink as the descending sun charged the wild cloud ranges outside with bright colour. The air was still. In the back of his mind he ran through his plan for the following day, but he became intensely aware of people, friends, being there with him. He talked to them and could not rationalise with himself that they were in fact figments of his oxygen-starved system, clinical apparitions. A girl with an aura of great warmth and companionship came close to him. He was strongly aware of her but when he looked directly at her she disappeared.

Messner slept heavily and the next morning, in a cloud of half-consciousness, he moved through curious layers of feeling: from comfortable security, resting there in the warm folds of his sleeping bag, to an acute sense of utter loneliness when the sharp reality of his position settled on him. He felt miserable under a bitter weight of depression. It had little now to do with Uschi but was pinned to a deeper, destructive feeling of isolation that he could no longer reconcile with a simple wish to climb mountains or to do something that no one else had done. The earthquake and the violence of the avalanche and the way the whole mountain below him had seemed to collapse went through his memory. Should he go back, concentrate his remaining strength on a safe retreat? No, he could not do that. He had come so far. Another day, just one more day.

Like some cold, glassy-eyed robot he climbed from the tent and instinctively checked the wind, the sharpness of the cold, the quality of the air and the clouds, all of which held small but significant clues to how the weather would be. Some distant peaks punctured the cloud sea and lay there like islands. It was seven o'clock. He looked up and there was the top, not too distant. If the snow and ice between his bivouac and the summit was firm, allowing his crampons to bite but not break the surface, he could be on the summit within four hours at the most.

But these hopes were quashed almost immediately he set off. The surface was soft and he sank up to his knees making it impossible to build the steady rhythm which would save energy and allow good progress. Sometimes he sank waist deep, gasping for breath, forcing himself from the cold grip of the snow. After three hours it was clear to him this was not a possible way to the summit. He would have to try another. The subtle internal gauge which would tell him that there was not enough strength remaining to reach the summit and escape alive was coming into action.

He stopped, crouched with his hands on his ice axe, looking up at the last defiant metres of Nanga Parbat. Without really rationalising his actions he crossed to a line of black rocks. It would be a last throw but they could at least give him a chance.

Crampon points rasped against the rocks, ice axe shaft clattered as his hands searched for holds. The points held. He moved up smoothly without sinking to his thighs. The dream suddenly became realisable again and the automaton took over. Muscles powered his body upwards without pain or fear. It was an instinctive action. The taps to his inner reserves of strength were open. He felt totally aware of what was happening and climbed with punctilious attention, breathing steadily, aware that clouds were now being torn across the sky in a wild parade. The horizon became endlessly distant and he had a strong feeling of detachment, a compound of tiredness and awareness that suddenly, alarmed, he realised could be dangerous. He looked for signs that he was becoming careless, irrational or hysterical but found none. He climbed higher, deliberately forcing air into his lungs by breathing quickly and deeply, wringing as much oxygen as he could from the thin atmosphere. "What am I doing here?" he asked himself. "Am I trying to escape from myself, cheat death, provoke fate, catch fame? No, none of this. I'm here because this is what I do best. This frozen, wind-blasted wilderness is me and I am part of it for this moment. Then I can emerge from it and describe it because people will want to know. I'm merely doing my job, a man on the move."

Advancing across the face of the summit block of Nanga Parbat, Messner watched the slow changes in light, colour and form projected by sun, wind and cloud along the summit ridge. The mountain was anchored so firmly yet all around there was swirling, unpredictable change and movement.

The ground continued to be steep and treacherously glazed with ice. Rock thrust out in small buttresses, gullies lay choked with hard ice. There were some cracks into which he could have driven a protective piton but he climbed on without hesitating. The act of climbing took care of itself; his lungs pumped oxygen into his blood cells to provide the energy for movement, his body balanced smoothly. The world shrank to the area immediately around him, to the next few holds and to moving over them securely. What was past was immediately forgotten. A hold that had been there a million or more years enjoyed that one instant of supporting a crampon point or a finger tip and was consigned back to negative oblivion.

A cliff of rock and ice more than 60 metres high slipped beneath him without his properly realising that it had been a cliff. To his right a line of rocks fell steeply from the summit. They would be easy ground but the traverse from where he stood was unthinkable without a partner. Could he use a peg to safeguard the move across? No; he rejected the temptation and trudged on up the more gently angled snow slope; taking a few steps, halting to gulp down more air and then pressing on. He began to know with certainty that he would reach the top. The sky, when he glanced upwards to squint at the final ridge, was empty blue-black space. He overcame another steep section; again, hold by hold, eroding the mountain like a caterpillar biting away at it dedicatedly and pugnaciously. Only 50 of 6,400 metres remained, but they were difficult. He stopped on a narrow ledge, pushed a lump of hard, Tyrolean bread into his parched mouth and chewed it around, feeling the saliva creeping back.

Immediately he had stopped climbing he became aware of the colossal exposure of the wall. The only way of countering that was to climb again. Once more the action was automatic, the only sound the scrape of crampon points on rock, the thump of his heart and the laboured sound of his breathing. It was intensely cold. The damp air of his breath immediately froze in the hair of his beard.

Occasionally Messner fixed his camera to the socket on his ice-axe and using the self-timer photographed himself scaling the face. It required hard, conscious effort to do even that simple act, consuming energy and valuable time. But it was a commercial necessity — a minting of money that would finance his next expedition and also provide objective proof of his achievements. But if the minutes he spent on it were to cost him his life, the photographs would be as useless up there as the gold of King Midas.

At four o'clock in the afternoon, everything depended on his reaching the top soon and finding a fast way down. The final ridge ended and there he was, gasping into his camera to prove his triumph. Visibility was sharply clear. He stood on the same point he had reached with Günther eight years earlier, from which they had made their tragic descent.

He felt calm. Even when he noticed and remembered the "gendarme" marking the point where he and Günther had emerged from the Rupal face on to the summit area, he remained calm. No outburst of emotion.

From his anorak he pulled an aluminium tube containing a copy of the first page of the Gutenberg Bible on which he wrote his name, the date and the route he had climbed. He buried the container in the rocks at the summit, photographed himself again and at 4.30 p.m. prepared to descend. Mist was beginning to swirl above the Diamir valley which was a splash of dark green that melted into the edge of the world. From that lofty perspective what appeared as huge peaks seen from the valley were dwarfed to insignificance.

Clouds were boiling in around Nanga Parbat 1,000 metres beneath him, swirling over the ridges. He ran a gloved hand over the ice at the summit. The mountain was so much a part of him, so wound into his life.

He started down, moving carefully along the south arête at first, then across the snow of the western corrie, his boots leaving dark heel marks in the snow. He felt profoundly tired but relieved that each step was now into air that was easier to breathe. He forced himself to be alert, to realise that he could not relax and that this was potentially the most dangerous part of the climb.

Weariness filled him. The ramp down which he was moving merged into a steep wall. He was too tired to return and find an easier way, yet a direct descent was not possible. His memory of the way he had descended with Günther was too blurred to be helpful. He searched for an alternative between the cliffs and snowfields below him. The way slowly unfolded and, exhausted, he reached the bivouac tent, clambered in and fell asleep. It was done.

Chapter 15

K2

VILLNÖSS WAS NOW more than ever a bolt hole from the intense pressure of his normal life. Messner's work on restoring the old house at St. Magdalena was complete and in between expeditions he based himself there writing, organising lectures, indexing the thousands of photographs he had acquired and planning the next adventure. What the people of the valley thought of him was difficult to guess. Having married Uschi — already divorced — and then, after their divorce, living with her occasionally at St. Magdalena, the neighbours were probably bewildered!

Reinhold felt that their relationship was happier now. Uschi had her freedom to work as she wanted and develop her own career writing for Bavarian television. He led his own impossibly busy life. When he returned from climbing Everest with Peter Habeler he packed 145 lectures into twelve weeks. In addition his book about the climb became an immediate best-seller and another strenuous lecture tour earned him almost one million Deutschmarks. Then after Nanga Parbat came another best-seller and yet another strenuous lecture tour. His lecture style was relaxed and informal. He drove around Germany in a scarlet Porsche to halls booked in advance by his publisher. He carried a battery of projectors which threw a pattern of four pictures on to the screen while he told the story of the climb from the front of the hall. The lectures were always to packed audiences and a lucrative session followed, autographing copies of his books. After his talks he always invited questions and these produced some useful information about what people thought and wanted to know about him. "Are you sure you are not mad?" one questioner asked after Nanga Parbat. "I don't think so but you are entitled to your opinion," came the calm reply.

Rarely did he have time to climb in the Alps since his sights were fixed on winning more of the 8,000 metre summits that had become the centre of his ambition. His friendship with Peter Habeler had ended when a book *Everest, Impossible Victory* had suddenly appeared on the market.

Reinhold had been unaware that Peter intended to write a book about their climb of Everest without oxygen and he had disapproved of some of the details he had included. There was no blazing row between the two men but Messner made it absolutely clear that Habeler would not be included in any of his future climbing plans. What he objected to, he said, was the way Habeler had dwelt on Messner's matrimonial problems. This may have been an over-reaction, but the book permanently fractured the close climbing relationship between the two of them.

It was paradoxical that the adventurous side of Messner's life, scaling Himalayan peaks by the most direct and difficult routes, was often less taxing than the coarser pressures of wheeling and dealing in his business life. He was a poor delegator, he admitted, and often his hands became impossibly full. He installed a housekeeper at Villnöss where the telephone rang continuously from early morning until late at night. There were journalists seeking stories; manufacturers of anything from wrist watches to underwear seeking to hitch their product to Messner's reputation; medical clinics wanting to examine him in detail for brain damage. . . . The demands were endless.

The Porsche covered big distances at high speed. Messner reflected that this was possibly the most dangerous part of his life, tearing along motorways between business appointments at the Fila factory near Milan, for instance, and BLV publishing house in Munich, with a lecture tour of 20 towns and cities to follow.

His contract with Fila was a simple arrangement. The company provided Messner with clothing and in return he was photographed upon the tips of an assortment of peaks dressed in climbing overalls manufactured by Fila or cutting his way up some precipitous slope with the company's logo prominently displayed on arm, leg or chest. Björn Borg was the other sporting star similarly under contract and the managing director of the company, a keen climber and Messner admirer, was able to report that Fila profits had more than doubled in one twelve-month period since starting the arrangement. Over the years Messner had been able to endorse a select number of products, and as a result his resources to back expeditions had increased sharply. He had no qualms about working to advertise products if that was one way of raising the funds to go climbing, adding to his income from books, films and lectures. It was fine for people with private means or government support to afford the high cost of expeditions. He was not in that position. Another way had to be found, it was as simple as that.

After his second ascent of Nanga Parbat, life became even more hectic and included the planning of an autumn trip with his Austrian climbing companions. They were to attempt a new route on Ama Dablam, the finely-shaped mountain which dominates Thyangboche Monastery on the way to Everest.

But before he could leave home, there was the future of the climbing school, that Messner had established and based in the Geisler Alps, to be discussed with the guides and instructors who ran the courses in his absence. This was a part of his life he was forced to delegate to others. Then there was equipment to select and organise and beyond that the plan for an expedition the following year to K2.

Messner's status as an internationally-known sporting figure brought a large number of visitors to St. Magdalena and the house beside the steep winding road. It was easily recognisable from the tall prayer flags flapping in the garden, relics of Everest Base Camp. He was not intolerant of the interest in him, the looks of searching calculation when he was recognised. What were the physical signs that this man was at all extraordinary? Was he powerfully built? — not at all, rather lean if anything. Had his hands grown huge from grappling with 8,000 metre giants? Not really — they were quite slender, sensitive, more the hands of an artist than someone who spent his life handling the raw elements of rock and ice.

From women the reaction was usually an inquisitive stare. Was there something darkly attractive about a man who lived constantly in the shadow of such danger, who thought perceptively about the motives for his adventures and wrote about them with great frankness?

His books demanded much work with his publisher in Munich and involved a team of ten people. Now there were revisions to be made on a new edition of *The Seventh Grade*, and a heap of invitations, requests, books and papers had arrived in the afternoon mail. The Messner household was easily the biggest customer for the Villnöss postal service. The small post-van groaned up the steep hill every day.

And even at night the telephone rang: some clinic in America perhaps seeking to measure his brain or monitor his heart, someone somewhere looking for a lecturer. But often the phone was ignored. Messner would go wearily to his bedroom where on the door was pinned a sign advising: "Avoid hangovers, stay drunk."

Early in 1979 permission came through for a six-strong Italian/Austrian expedition to attempt K2. In the early summer they arrived in Rawalpindi only to face almost a fortnight of delays because of bad weather which had cut off surface communication with Skardu in the Upper Indus valley. Messner smiled at the slick way this expedition had been organised. One day he had been busily finishing off half a dozen tasks that were urgent. Then after a couple of hours down in the cellar of his house at St. Magdalena selecting equipment from the neatly stacked heaps of climbing gear, he was ready. It was almost as easy as preparing for a climb in the Alps.

The first injury of the expedition was suffered in the hotel swimming pool in Rawalpindi. Renato Casarotto performed a dive that was too spectacular for the depth of water and surfaced with burst lips and barely conscious.

Eventually the climbers were offered a lift to Skardu in a Pakistani Hercules transport plane. They piled in their three tons of equipment and in a few hours were standing on the rubble-strewn landing strip at Skardu in wet, unpleasant weather. They hired 120 porters whose services cost a total of DM 65,000. Inflation and rising expectations had reached the Himalayas, Messner thought. Thank heavens this was only a small expedition. Even so the total cost of the climb would now be well over DM 204,000. It was difficult to calculate what it would nowadays have cost the Japanese team who climbed K2 in 1977 using shifts of 42 mountaineers. The previous year an American expedition had placed four of its twelve climbers on the summit and had paid over DM 1,400,000 for the privilege.

The Italian/Austrian team arrived hoping to attempt what Messner described as the "magic line" up this highly complex peak. K2 rises more than eight kilometres high, a great angular pyramid of rock bounded by six distinct ridges or spurs. The most famous of these was named after the Duke of the Abruzzi who explored there early this century. Most of the eleven attempts were by this obvious ridge which was climbed by the Italians in 1954 and a Japanese party three years later. The North-East Ridge was climbed by the four Americans in 1978 but K2's forbidding size had always attracted only large and well-sponsored expeditions.

Messner walked ahead of the porters through the dark countryside of the Braldo along the track that he could well recall taking with Peter Habeler on their climb of Hidden Peak. From the rough path he could see the river roaring powerfully in the bed of the gorge. He glanced down and noticed a speck of colour among a group of boulders on the opposite bank. He looked closer and discovered with a shock that it was a human corpse jammed in the rocks at the side of the river. The waters were low at that time. There was nothing anyone could do to retrieve the body which would anyway shortly be covered when the river level rose. Enquiry revealed that the body could only be that of an Englishman who was lost the previous year when he had fallen in.

With this grim reminder of how dangerous even the approach to the mountain could be, the small group continued towards the Baltoro Glacier with their heavily-laden line of porters. At the end of the column was a major in the Pakistan Army who acted as liaison officer and interpreter and kept a close watch to ensure that the climbers did not photograph either military installations or women, or install any spying devices aimed across the Chinese border.

They were now among the highest mountains with Masherbrum, Chogolisa, Gasherbrum, Broad Peak and the Muztagh Tower rising around them from the cold, bleached bones of glacier ice. Beyond towered the massive pyramid of K2, only two rope lengths lower than Everest. How, Messner wondered, would they fare?

They had already been delayed by an unfortunate accident to Ursula Grether who badly injured an ankle and had to be carried down to the village of Askole by Messner and Friedl Mutschlechner. The injury was so bad that Ursula had to return to Germany.

The Godwin-Austen glacier steepened where it branched away towards K2 from the broken, grey artery of the Baltoro. The cold pinched harder as the air became thinner. The porters struggling under their heavy loads grew more miserable and demanded more money. Perhaps they thought themselves to be in a stronger bargaining position when there were so few sahibs around. Their complete demoralisation was sealed when one porter fell 15 metres into a crevasse and was killed. The ice simply opened up under him, and he disappeared. Friedl Mutschlechner followed by Robert Schauer, a medical student, abseiled into the concealed abyss and found the body, confirming that Ali Quasir from the village of Shigar had died instantly when he hit the bottom.

The porters refused to climb any further up the Savoia glacier, where the accident occurred. Instead they turned hastily back towards the safer ground of the Godwin-Austen glacier where Base Camp was established. Another name was added to those on the memorial cairn at the foot of K2 — the grim tally of lives lost on the mountain.

Messner was angry about this turn of events. Without a Base Camp much higher up the Savoia glacier beneath the South Face, there would be no possibility of attacking his ''magic line'' which traced an elegant path across the face to the summit. But he set off alone to see for himself whether the theory he had mapped out on a photograph in Villnöss was confirmed by reality on the mountainside. Swiftly he threaded his way up the glacier past the remains of the American and British Base Camps to the point where his pencil had begun to trace its line. It had not been entirely a fantasy inscribed on a photograph. From Hidden Peak in 1975 he had noted this possible route which had stood out sharply, catching his attention as he looked across to the isolated face. It had looked superb but seen from near at hand the reality was sharply different. Distance had quite definitely lent enchantment and there was no connection between his theories and the reality which on close acquaintance lost all its magic. The southern pillar and the entire wall to its left was threatened by a huge icefall. What had appeared from a distance to be a series of small hollows of compacted snow was in fact the leading edge of a hanging glacier which would inevitably send a heavy and unpredictable barrage of broken ice directly on to the route. Jagged edges of freshly broken ice were clearly to be seen. Messner calculated the chances in his mind. There was always some risk at certain points in an icefall but it could generally be concentrated into a relatively short section and minimised by moving quickly past, early in the day when the ice was still well-consolidated. Here the situation was quite different. The ice would fall from the southern pillar over a considerable portion of the route. The climbers would require several hours to clear the section and would have to cross it time and time again to supply the upper pitches.

He realised that to place the expedition there would be not only Russian roulette, but Russian roulette with all but one chamber loaded. The route was impossibly dangerous. There was no alternative on the south-west side and from the Savoia glacier the South Pillar and the area around it was more broken than he had judged from the photographs.

In the light of these discoveries, Alessandro Gogna and Renato Casarotto now formed a two-man reconnaissance team which went round to the eastern side of the mountain and the Abruzzi Ridge where they found, hidden by deep, fresh snow, the remains of the Japanese camps and a trove of whisky, oxygen, boiled ham and tinned seaweed. Beneath the snow there were also great lengths of rope leading up the ridge. It seemed clear that the Japanese had secured much of this route with fixed ropes and occasionally substantial lengths of aluminium ladder.

In the meantime, Michl Dacher and Robert Schauer went up the Savoia Glacier on skis and, reaching the area Reinhold had examined from a distance, confirmed his doubts about the southern face.

Reinhold, with Friedl Mutschlechner, turned to exploring the face overlooking the Godwin-Austen glacier and picked out a line running through the ice-covered steepness of the wall in a fairly direct path towards the Abruzzi Ridge. Reinhold casually remarked that this wall could prove a potential solo route. He had already suggested that he might possibly try a solo trip if they failed as a team on the "magic line". But his five partners had reacted strongly, worried that Messner planned to use the expedition as a springboard for another solo epic, leaving them in the role of assistants.

He and Mutschlechner spent the night in a bivouac tent close to the start of the new line. They began to explore the climb together early the next day but after 200 metres Messner arrived at the edge of a snow hollow through which the route would have had to pass. For the second time he found that he was looking into a no-go area. The hollow was steeply tilted and filled with fresh snow. It would inevitably be slow going to cross on to the better ground on the far side and throughout that time they would be threatened by a line of ice towers poised like rickety skyscrapers immediately above the bowl. The objective danger during the crossing would be far too high. Yet another option had been checked out and discarded. K2 was proving an impregnable fortress to the small expedition!

The following day all the climbers returned to their Base Camp on the Godwin-Austen glacier. They were despondent, realising that their ambitious plans prepared 10,000 kilometres away on the basis of photographs had not worked out.

Reinhold spoke to his companions, admitting that none of the projected routes was viable and that there was no alternative to the traditional Abruzzi Ridge, climbed originally by the Duke of Abruzzi in 1909 to a height of 6,700 metres. He proposed that they should repeat the old route in a new style; fast, without oxygen and by a uniquely small expedition. That was all they could hope to salvage from their original plans.

He became enthusiastic and very positive. "It will be the first time that such an eight-thousander has been climbed in this way," he said; "it will be like making six solo ascents at the same time." Robert Schauer agreed. It would be the only way of preserving a chance to reach the summit. Friedl Mutschlechner, who had seen the condition of the south face, said that at best they would wear themselves out and take unjustifiable risks if they attempted the South Pillar. Reinhold himself firmly rejected the idea of even starting to attempt his "magic line". He was aware of his reputation for putting the lives of people in danger, of being so much in a class of his own that he could survive where others perished. His companions did not believe this newspaper image. A small expedition to a big mountain was a dangerous game but the responsibility for tragedy, if it happened, was borne by the group and not pinned to a particular person. Each man had his own skill and ability to survive; it was up to him to ensure that he did not step beyond the bounds of reason. Reinhold was not urging any of them to do so, but what Alessandro Gogna, Robert Schauer and Renato Casarotto had questioned was that he might suddenly decide to make a solo bid for the summit leaving them holding the safety net at the bottom. He assured them that this was not his intention and that no solo attempt would be made by anyone until there had been a combined assault on the mountain.

As they debated their plans there was a thundering explosion outside the tent and a huge slab of the south wall broke free and crashed down towards the Savoia Glacier sending a fall-out of ice spume and a violent pressure wave that they could feel in Base Camp. Any remaining hopes that there might be some possible route up the wall ended at that moment.

Casarotto, one of the finest technical climbers in the world, with some spectacular solo ascents in the Andes to his credit, reflected that it would surely be better to return home having failed on some new line and not reached the top rather than merely repeat the old route. It was the argument Messner himself had used on Everest. If conditions were bad it was surely better to fail on the impossible rather than on what everyone knew was possible, except that the significance could lie in the method just as much as in the route they chose.

The debate ended with everyone agreeing to attempt the Abruzzi Ridge which curved up the northern crest of the mountain. The last few days of June were spent setting up a Base of bright red tents at the foot of the ridge as the first climbers set off up the route. Signs of previous occupation were abundant and as the wind strengthened to storm force an old Japanese oxygen bottle even whistled past Robert Schauer's head. He and Friedl Mutschlechner spent a sleepless night on the ridge before returning to Base Camp.

On June 30 Gogna climbed alone to Camp II at 6,600 metres — the point which had been Camp IV on the first successful K2 expedition in 1954. Renato Casarotto followed Gogna with difficulty because he was suffering from the effects of altitude and a hacking, bronchial cough. Gogna reported by radio to Base Camp that his companion was feeling "multo limpido" and, if he did not begin to show signs of recovery the following day, he would head down the mountain. The wind howled in from China shaking their tiny tent on its precarious perch.

The work on preparing the route, often utilising ropes and aluminium

Left: Training at Villnöss

Above: The house at Villnöss: training among the prayer-flags

Messner's house at Villnöss

The view down the valley from the house

View across the meadow to Messner's cabin

The cabin that he built unaided

At K2 Base Camp – the mountain in the background

Left: Messner and Habeler after their "oxygen-free" ascent of Everest in 1978

Right: Wolfgang Nairz, leader of the 1978 Austrian Everest expedition

Below: Everest showing the South Col, 1978

1978 Everest expedition: return to Base Camp, snow-blind

A warm greeting from Ursula Grether

Everest from the North

The ruins of the Rongbuk monastery on the
northern approaches to Everest, 1980

Above: Nena Holguin
boarding the aircraft
for China

Left: Alone at the summit
of Everest

ladders left by the Japanese, continued for about two weeks. Reinhold's hands were covered in blisters from hammering in fresh pitons. The atmosphere on the mountainside was one of brooding greyness. The ridge was infinitely more difficult than the "via normale" on Everest and the climbers became aware that if anyone was injured, there could be no hope of rescue. Even a simple injury could in effect be fatal.

They prepared three camps on the ridge, and the final section from 7,400 metres would have to be covered in one day or by using a bivouac. The first summit pair were Messner and Michl Dacher, a short, dark and wiry man from Piting in Upper Bavaria who worked as a power cable engineer. He was aged 45, the oldest climber on the expedition, but quite as stubbornly determined as his partner. He had already climbed Kangchenjunga and Lhotse, the third and fourth highest summits in the world. Messner's own record was at this time five 8,000 metre peaks.

In the bivouac tent at 7,910 metres early on July 8 the two climbers lay half asleep, their breath turning to hoar frost and plastering the tent walls. The tough shelter had been dug well into a steep slope and pinned down with ropes secured to ice screws. Outside the ground fell away precipitously to the Godwin-Austen Glacier. At 2 a.m. Reinhold poked his head from the thick folds of his sleeping bag through which he could sense the intense cold of the outside world.

"Michl, we must cook," he said.

Dacher pondered on this a little. The "we" had rather suggested it might be a joint effort but the expedition leader already had the look of someone fast asleep. Dacher emerged reluctantly and opened the end of the tunnel-tent to shovel some snow into a pan. The cold outside had a barbaric quality, biting at his hand and freezing the circulation. He lit the stove and climbed back into the warm folds of the sleeping bag. The sound of the pan spitting and hissing woke them up. They made soup and waited until the wind started to die down. Shortly after 5 a.m. the sun penetrated the tent without warmth and the two men slipped out of their sleeping bags and into their down suits. Outside the tent they pulled on overboots, fastened crampons tightly and set out on the final 700 metres to the summit. The time was 7 a.m. and the keen wind had moderated enough to allow safe progress.

The first slope was deceptively easy. Dacher felt irrationally optimistic, ignoring the way the head of the mountain reared up steeply above them. At the first steep slope they halted, confronted by an incline of bottomless soft snow, part of the same fall that had plastered other mountains of North Pakistan and bogged down the hopes of several expeditions.

They waded upwards, floundering like a couple of short-legged animals. Messner was concerned that if the slope avalanched they would be carried down to the Godwin-Austen glacier far below them. They floundered rather more gingerly.

In due course, the slope narrowed to a gully full of ice-glazed rock and beyond that to a 30-metre high wall. In the Dolomites, Messner thought, it would be perhaps grade three but here at 8,200 metres with the thin air and a jet-stream wind befuddling and freezing the brain it was a damned sight harder.

There was no way of circumventing the wall. They tried to move up the slopes on either side but were forced back. Michl Dacher, grinning at his partner behind his small, round goggles, cleared a ledge on the wall with his ice axe. This allowed a little extra height for reaching a snow slope on the left. Once again the surface was soft, waist deep and highly dangerous. The slope rose endlessly. The two climbers fought to move and to breathe. Reinhold's altimeter read 8,350 metres.

A hundred metres more and the snow still remained deep; it had the quality of a steep, cold quicksand. Messner hoped grimly that the sky would remain clear. It was already 3 p.m. and they had no chance now of reaching the shelter of the bivouac tent before dark. If they were to reach safety it would be by moonlight.

The two men took turns at forcing a track through the soft snow. The movement was quite divorced from the easy, skilfully swift action of normal climbing. It was a torturing, hard slog, each man keeping going but waiting hopefully for the other to give in. The partnership became a curious, grim competition, neither saying a word. They reached the summit almost without comment, feeling only a great gratitude that there was nothing further to climb. The weather remained relatively calm; the cold was intense, covering their beards with a hoary whiteness of frozen breath. They suffered no hallucinations, no outbursts of feeling. For Messner and Dacher another 8,000 metre summit had been added to their collections.

The tracks led like dark scars in the moonlit snow down to the bivouac. There was a calmness about the mountain that was almost ethereal. They slept well and the next day descended through the various camps as conditions once again deteriorated. Heavy snow and high winds wiped out any further possibility of another attempt, which was deeply frustrating to the rest of the team. They had worked well together and as they departed down the Godwin-Austen glacier, a French expedition of classic size was starting to arrive at the Base Camp area. Before he left Reinhold noted that there were more men in the television team filming the French attempt than in the whole of his own expedition. As the French tents rose to form a noisy town on the glacier edge, he reflected wryly that where expeditions were concerned, small really was beautiful.

The expedition to Ama Dablam in October 1979 was to have been a small-scale attempt on that most beautiful Himalayan peak. With Messner was a group of companions from Everest including Wolfgang Nairz, Bulle Ölz and Horst Bergman. They would try the regular route that was first climbed illegally in 1963. Also on the mountain was a team of four New Zealanders attempting the west face. The Austrians could pick out the others higher up the mountain. The tragedy happened with sudden violence. There was an explosion as an avalanche broke free and swept down the face directly above the New Zealanders. They could not escape the full weight of the frozen deluge.

Belays were torn out. Bodies were hurled down the steep face. When the avalanche subsided two climbers, Peter Hillary and Merv English, were hanging from one slender belay. The other pair, Ken Hislop and Geoff Gabities, had fallen on top of them and their rope had snagged across Peter Hillary's waist. Peter lay on the rope, the weight of the other two causing agony to fractures in his left arm and right ankle. Geoff had a deep rope-burn that exposed the bone in one arm. Merv had not been too badly hurt but Ken had been in the most vulnerable position and had taken the full force of the avalanche. He had sustained terrible head injuries and must have been killed outright. All that Geoff could do was to cut the rope.

The three began a painful retreat watched from below by the Austrians. A helicopter was summoned and the climbers set off up the south-west ridge to try to help the New Zealanders from above. The plan did not work and the following day the Austrians climbed to the high camp the other team had been using, carrying equipment and fixed ropes for the rescue.

Reinhold and Bulle stayed there the night and at 6 am set out to meet the New Zealanders. They climbed so quickly, they covered in five hours what had taken the others two days. The helicopter arrived but could not reach the injured men. It would return the following day to the high camp. By then, Reinhold and Bulle had fixed ropes and shepherded the New Zealanders to safety. The Austrians had lost any chance of reaching the summit themselves but that was a small price to pay for three lives.

Chapter 16

EVEREST ALONE

"IT WILL BE possible to have the interview on December 5 on the train leaving Hanover at 7.40 a.m. for Hamburg. Your seat has been booked — C21 in carriage 15; Herr Messner will be next to you in seat C22." The publicity department at Messner's publishing house in Munich had slotted me into the programme with almost a parody of German precision. I would have approximately one hour and 45 minutes for my "interview"; then Reinhold would be going to a lunch provided by the manufacturers of a brand of "magic drops" that he had used on his latest expedition. One spot of this liquid, I later discovered, taken on the tip of the tongue, acted like a powerful drain cleaner on any sinus or nasal passage that happened to be blocked. After the lunch and a lecture on the efficacy of the magic drops Reinhold would be returning to Hanover. During that journey yet another journalist had arranged to hold an interview with him from the neighbouring seat. In the evening there was to be a lecture on the K2 expedition at Hanover University. All the seats had been sold. Reinhold would then be going to bed, ready to begin another identical programme in another part of Germany the following day. As a way of life it seemed the exact opposite of the slow, remote act of climbing to a Himalayan summit and I was anxious to see him at work in this different context.

With three minutes to spare I caught the train. Reinhold was there in seat C22, as friendly as ever and, for a man strapped to such a millwheel of a lecture tour, very relaxed.

"You know," he said, "they all want me to continue being the great mountain climber, in good condition and pursuing great adventures; yet they also want me to be sitting in their offices, cutting films or writing articles and books." Maintaining equilibrium between such demands was difficult.

In seat C23 was Nena Holguin, Messner's companion; an amiable Canadian with the same restless enthusiasm. Accompanying him on a

European lecture tour, she said, was like putting your feet in fire: forty days and nights in an urban wilderness of lecture halls, hotels, restaurants and offices. There were the thousands of faces, autographs and questions but the reward they appreciated most was the response from ordinary folk who perhaps would never dream of climbing a mountain but who could nevertheless respect the achievement. However, providing surrogate adventure was hard on the nerves.

"He often wonders why he feels compelled to work so hard. He says 'I have enough money; I could take it easy,' but his system is like an engine that thrives on high revs," Nena says.

It was hard to stay cool on these crazy lecture circuits, she confessed: "There is an appointment now in a place 50 kilometres away but the roads are covered in snow. By the way, a journalist from Frankfurt will be coming to the hotel at 2 p.m., and then they must go directly to the hall for the lecture. While I am setting up the projectors and discovering both that the leads are not long enough and the screen is too narrow, Reinhold is outside meeting a publisher. Then there are the last two chapters of the new edition of *The Seventh Grade* to read through before bed and it is already past midnight. There will be no time in the morning because there are already two appointments fixed."

Reinhold's lean face showed the strain. Back at Funes in the quiet old farmhouse the mail would already be stacked in neat piles two feet high — the yield of interest which his adventures and lectures had generated. One half of him felt gratified by the response, the other half sensed that he had constructed an elaborate treadmill for his personal use. Not all the reaction was flattering. Some correspondents, like the questioners at his lectures, clearly doubted that he was altogether sane to lay his life on the line quite so often. In the papers and on TV other critics, unlikely ever to put a boot on Everest themselves, had poured a cold shower of mockery on what they saw as his extreme antics in the mountains. I particularly recalled Clive James' thoughts on *Everest Unmasked*, the television film of the first climb without oxygen. They had been noteworthy although they gave no credit to the achievement:

"Up they strove o'er col and cwm. 'This is what separates the men from the boys,' warned the voice-over. Playing strange instruments, monks in lonely monasteries placated the gods. Hoo-woo. Bong. Sherpas loyally fell into crevasses. One of them was crushed to death 150ft under an icefall. Another had to be brought down on a stretcher and sewn back together. Obviously the sheer volume of tourist traffic is tempting the previously sure-footed Sherpas to work hazardously long hours, despite the guidelines laid down by their union, NUTCASE — the Nepalese Union of Trained Climbers Assisting Suicidal Expeditions.

"Reinhold made it to the top. But the peril was not over. There was still the danger of brain damage — or, in Reinhold's case, further brain damage. The chances were that this would first manifest itself in the form of burst blood-vessels in the eyeball, loss of memory, impaired speech functions and the sudden, irrational urge to participate in stupid television programmes. Most of these symptoms duly appeared. Nevertheless Reinhold's achievement could not be gainsaid. He and his friends had proved that it is not enough to risk your neck. It is in the nature of man to risk his brains as well. Fighting his way upwards through drifts of empty beer cans and Kentucky Fried Chicken cartons, Reinhold had added his name to the select few thousand who have conquered the Lonely Mountain."

For Messner, climbing Everest alone was both an outrageous idea and a logical step. His plan was to arrive on the Chinese side of Everest with his rucksack and his girl friend, and, without help or artificial oxygen, climb to the top of the mountain and back alone — a simple, ascetic and spectacular feat. He had previously ruled out such a solo ascent as impossible, even after he had climbed Everest from the south in 1978. The fine membrane separating acceptable risk and certain death would, he thought, have been stretched too far. A climber faced with the huge, oxygen-starved expanse of Everest could not survive however determined he was. But his solo climb of Nanga Parbat had changed his mind. The Diamir flank was more complex and technically harder than either the north or south ridges of Everest, and though Everest towered higher than Nanga Parbat, when Messner judged his performance there against the extra height of Everest he decided that given good luck and fair weather he could do it.

There was another driving force: competition. Messner heard that the Japanese mountaineer Naomi Uemura planned a solo attempt and was applying for permission. The risk that the most coveted "first" in mountaineering might be lost was too great.

In April 1980, therefore, Reinhold had flown to Peking to negotiate permission to climb Minja Kongur, since he had scant hope of securing Everest for a solo attempt. The authorities explained that the Kongur permission had been given to Chris Bonington.

"How about Everest in the monsoon months?" Messner enquired. To his surprise the Chinese official agreed. He was very courteous and helpful although his considerateness did not extend to the fee for the doubtful privilege of attempting Everest alone. A French team had been given permission for the post-monsoon period and Messner negotiated first refusal should the French back down. He had also provisionally "booked" the mountain from the Nepalese side, although he did not relish the prospect of attempting any of those routes alone. The South Col route which he had climbed with Peter Habeler two years earlier contained the extremely dangerous Khumbu Icefall and the West Ridge included some very hard climbing. Easily the most feasible solo route would lie up the North Ridge. During the monsoon it was hardly a soft option but Messner had been told that there could be slightly more shelter on that side of the mountain and also that a ten-day lull of fine weather could be expected in the middle of every monsoon.

Within a week the permission had been arranged. The attempt would cost $50,000, cheap compared with the $2m. it had cost the Japanese to climb the same ridge. The Chinese had opened their mountains as a gesture of friendship but they were clearly intent on raising as much foreign currency from the gesture as possible. The authorities insisted that Messner take with him an interpreter, a liaison officer and a medical officer who would wait at base camp. Messner assured them that the first-aid certificate that Nena Holguin held would be sufficient.

Before they set out Reinhold asked Nena what she would do if he did not reappear at base camp.

"A lot will depend," said Nena, "on how things look on the mountain. If it is stormy I will allow you a good two or three days after the storm lets up. I will not go up alone to help you because I know that you do not want that unless I can see you near the North Col or below. If there is no sign of you I guess first of all I would go down to Base Camp and see if Cheng would come up to help me look for you. But we would not be able to go very high. The best thing I could do then would be to try and rush a message to Lhasa and ask for a helicopter to come and search for you. It would not be easy. I'm sure I would have to go to Lhasa myself and beg and pay in advance for a helicopter. But I would try my best even if it took two months before they began looking. In any case I would never give up on you, Reinhold, even if I had to come back some day with my own expedition. I'd look for you until I found you."

Reinhold listened to her carefully and grinned.

"Yes, you're right. That would be the best thing you could do. I'm happy that you know how to act. There would be no sense in your climbing up there and dying too."

Nena said: "I know. If I die who will look for you? I'm much more helpful if I'm alive."

The North Ridge of Everest is historically a "British" climb. All the first attempts in the 1920s and 1930s went this way and it was here that Mallory and Irvine disappeared in 1924. Messner had read the early accounts closely. He had become a great admirer of the British pioneers who had almost succeeded without any of the equipment and technical skills that modern climbers could call on.

"Those men were very great mountaineers," he said. "I am amazed still at the thought of Odell wandering up and down the North Face and Colonel Norton reaching so close to the summit, all of them wearing nailed boots and often without oxygen equipment, although it is doubtful the equipment they had would have been much help anyway."

On June 29 Messner's small caravan of one jeep and a half-loaded truck left Lhasa for the camp near the Rongbuk monastery; four people bouncing over the empty Tibetan landscape bound for the highest mountain in the world. The team seemed ludicrously small compared with the long cavalcade of climbers and porters and tons of equipment that normally constituted an Everest attempt.

When they reached Rongbuk they saw that the building was in ruins. The site they chose for their camp had last been used by a British expedition, probably in the 1920s. Messner found it by comparing early photographs with the landscape near the glacier. It was hidden away, and clearly no one had camped there for many years. They found scraps of British newspapers relating to one of the attempts during the 1920s, though they were hardly readable and had been stuck to the wall perhaps out of remembrance.

Messner saw that Everest from the north was a totally different mountain from the one now familiar to European expeditions. It was huge and sprawling with the lower half of the route hidden by an intervening rise, but with the higher reaches, where Mallory and Irvine had disappeared, clearly in sight and covered with snow. One glance told him that the mountain was in an impossible condition for climbing.

They hired three yaks and two drivers to transport their equipment from Rongbuk at 5,100 metres to the foot of the North Col at 6,500 metres where they made a high camp. They completed this move in three days beginning on July 13.

Whilst they waited for the weather to clear they explored some of the valleys in the area and planned to stay at some of the villages the British climbers had described in the pre-revolution days. They found that most of these settlements now lay in ruins or were deserted. Nomads still wandered over the region although the prayer flags that once fluttered in the wind throughout Tibet were now replaced by the red flags of China.

The weather was still poor with heavy snow falling on the mountain and a relatively high temperature that made the slope leading up to the North Col too dangerous. So Reinhold and Nena explored up the central Rongbuk glacier and bivouacked at 6,000 metres. The following day they hoped to cross to the edge of the Lho Lha, where George Mallory had stood and looked down for the first time into the Western Cwm, but the snow was thigh-deep and too exhausting.

Reinhold tried once to reach the North Col from the advance base, wallowing waist-deep up slopes of wet snow that threatened to avalanche. It was here that seven Sherpas had died on the 1922 expedition. He reached a wide crevasse dividing the slope from the Col and from this vantage point he could see that the ridge beyond was still plastered with snow. There could be no chance yet of attempting the climb until the temperature had fallen sufficiently to freeze the surface. Messner felt disheartened by the possibility that in the monsoon months the weather might not clear up in time for him to make an attempt.

Two weeks, and local weather lore proved exactly right. The sky cleared and when they returned to Rongbuk from a recce of Shisha Pangma, a high peak that Messner also had permission to explore, they noticed that a small pool near the camp was frozen hard. The wind had died away and the air had a sharp, brittle quality. The ''weather window'' they had hoped for had arrived and loose snow on the high ridge had been blown away. To Messner it seemed that two monsoons sweeping up from the Gulf of Bengal and the Persian Gulf had met immediately above Everest and were between them holding back the clouds.

On August 16 Reinhold and Nena reached advance base in fast time. The steep snow slope leading to the North Col was in perfect condition now: crisp, firm and yielding enough to give a positive grip. On the 17th he started out in a pair of jogging shoes instead of boots and carrying the rucksack he would need for his attempt the following day. The slope was so firm that he virtually ran up it to the lip of the crevasse below the North Col. He put in an ice screw and clipped his rucksack to it, and then returned to advance base. His idea was to give himself a quick lightweight start the next day.

The rucksack weighed about 20 kilos and contained a small bivouac tent, a sleeping bag and a plastic mattress. His ice axe and crampons were made of titanium for lightness. There was also a stove, spare mitts and goggles. His food supplies were thin strips of beef, dried fruit, chocolate, sardines, tomato soup and Tibetan salt tea. His ice axe again had a screw fitting into which he could fix his camera to photograph himself while climbing.

At 5 a.m. on August 18 he dressed in his light down climbing suit and pulled on his plastic boots. The sky outside was clear, the air still. He set off. "I'll be thinking about you," Nena called. Reinhold did not catch what she said. "What?" he asked brusquely. "Bye-bye," she said. It sounded a very inadequate bon voyage.

In the pitch darkness his head torch picked out the ice slope, a solitary circle of light on the vastness of Everest. He felt fit and mentally prepared for the climb, moving quickly up the firm slope. He reached the crevasse below the North Col in 90 minutes, an hour faster than the best Mallory had recorded. He felt totally determined, his mind focused on the ascent ahead and his body reacting automatically to the technical procedure of climbing. He picked up the rucksack and slipped it over his shoulders. The snow was so firm that he did not fit the crampons to his boots.

In the darkness he could pick out the top of the crevasse he had to cross — another crevasse, one of thousands he had negotiated during his 2,000 climbs. His body launched smoothly across the five-foot gap but something was wrong. He was falling, in slow motion it seemed, into the empty blackness below the lip. His head torch sent tumbling swathes of light across the walls of blue ice. He was out of control.

There was no fear, no thought that he might die. He remembered thinking, "If you get out of this you must go home, somewhere safe." The fall stopped. He was lying on a snow bridge about eight metres down the crevasse, unhurt, hardly bruised. His helmet lamp was out but in the cold darkness above him he could pick out the stars, shining through the entrance to the crevasse. The shock came to him then. Would the bridge give way sending him deeper into the heart of the glacier?

Then a sense of control flooded back. He got his lamp working again and saw a ramp leading upwards from the lower end of the bridge. He worked his way towards it and within minutes was on the surface but still on the downhill side of the crevasse. Hardly hesitating, he pushed his two ski sticks into the slope on the other side of the gap and using them as security stepped across. He realised then that in his first attempt the edge of the crevasse had collapsed. His wish to go home, to return to somewhere safe, had already gone. His mind was focused once more on climbing Everest.

He checked his watch. In spite of the accident he had been climbing only two hours and it was still pitch dark.

Half an hour later the sun rose quickly, flooding the mountain with bright snow-reflected light and shrinking the dark shadows on the north face. The steady momentum of the climb brought back a feeling of great confidence and the perfect snow allowed him to move swiftly until his altimeter read nearly 7,000 metres.

The surface had softened and Messner found that his boots sank deeper into the snow, demanding extra energy. In the thin air this signalled a gasping surge of effort. He had been consuming Everest at the phenomenal rate of more than 300 metres an hour. The mountain was completely snow covered and the only sign that anyone had been there before him was a short length of red climbing rope which appeared from the snow and then disappeared into it again. Any other secrets the face held were hidden from him beneath a thick white carpet.

He had carefully gone into the history of Everest and was greatly intrigued by the mystery of Mallory and Irvine and the possibility that they had died *after* reaching the summit. He studied the ridge above him closely and concluded that, because of the great technical difficulties he could see clearly on the Second Step below the summit and the times mentioned in Odell's last report of them, it was extremely unlikely that the two climbers could have reached the top and returned. The most likely explanation, Messner thought, was that they had died somewhere between the First and Second Steps while still on the way up, near the point where an ice axe had been found by a later expedition.

Approaching about 8,000 metres Messner reached a small rock platform where he put up a tent and ate a meal of cold dried beef strips and salt tea. He still felt fit despite having climbed almost 1,500 metres that day. The only sign of high altitude was again a strong sense that there was another person with him. He divided his meal into two and made a second mug of salt tea. He even felt annoyed that his one-man tent was desperately overcrowded with two people in it. But he slept well in his lonely eyrie, more than satisfied with his progress and counting his good luck that the weather had held clear and the wind was relatively light.

The next day, August 19, he packed up his tent and prepared to climb. "I move like a snail with my home on my back," he thought, "going slowly from place to place, going steadily but always going."

Immediately above the camp site the ridge reared steeply. When he tried to climb, his boots sank into the snow and he wasted two hours exploring various approaches to the edge of the ridge. Away to his right the north face of Everest stretched in a long slope that was scarred by old avalanches. The only direction that gave any chance of upward progress was a diagonal traverse of this slope. For hours he inched his way across the face, aware that any new avalanche would sweep him to oblivion. He moved delicately, careful not to disturb any hidden trigger that might set off another fall.

By late afternoon he had covered nearly two kilometres from his last camp but was less than 400 metres higher up the mountain. All the same, he had crossed once again into the so-called "death zone". He set up his bivouac tent on a mushroom of snow which he hoped would shield him from any new avalanches. Above him the long gulley of the Norton Couloir pointed towards the summit.

Messner was depressed by his slight progress that day. The long traverse had taken an eternity and had brought him little closer to his goal. He felt tired and with difficulty summoned the energy to warm up some soup and to force liquid into his system. He was uneasy and could not sleep. The next morning his spirits fell further still as he watched clouds swirling in from the east. An hour later snow started to fall. Perhaps he was too late. The locals had been right, the spell of good mid-monsoon weather had lasted exactly ten days. Today was the eleventh.

He left the tent, sleeping bag and all his stores and started up the couloir. Snow swirled around him but through occasional breaks in the cloud he could see down to the Rongbuk glacier. He felt the benefit of not having his rucksack; the snail without its shell moved at a faster crawl but was more vulnerable. The couloir was choked with snow and where it steepened at a distinctive band of yellow rock Messner broke out to the right, climbing towards the North Pillar of Everest which he could see had been stripped of snow by the wind. A ramp led from the yellow band of rock to the upper section of the pillar.

He was moving fairly quickly again but the mountain seemed to be stretching on for ever. Visibility fell to 50 metres. A high band of black rock suddenly blocked his progress. Which way? Instinctively he moved to the left and found a break in the cliff that he could climb. Through the mist the last snow pyramid appeared. He was exhausted now and moved only a few slow steps at a time before stopping to gulp air into his lungs.

Shortly after three o'clock he caught sight of the tripod that the Chinese had put to mark the summit. The snow had built up around it so that only the top 30 centimetres of metal were showing.

"I felt very quiet, very tired," Messner was to record later. "I sat there for more than half an hour. I took some photographs and I had no fear about getting down. It was very peaceful.'' One man alone on top of the world.

At about four o'clock Messner left the summit. His footprints were still clear and guided him down but his body, robbed of sleep, starved of oxygen and exhausted by the effort of climbing Everest alone, was spent, his mind numbed. He reached his high camp in about three-and-a-half hours and shuffled clumsily into the sleeping bag. He did not have the energy to light the stove to make a drink even though his throat was parched. He lay there crippled with exhaustion, with no will to move but unable to sleep.

That night represented the ultimate assault on his willpower. He lay in the small bivouac tent, totally spent. Normally, his body responded, if only sluggishly, to the powers of recovery inculcated by so many climbs, so much cold and an infinity of subdued fear. But this time it was different; he had climbed Everest quite by himself without help. No bottled oxygen or lines of load carriers, no chain of camps strung below him down the mountain like some nurturing umbilical cord. Only Nena, no doubt lying anxiously awake in the small camp some 2,000 metres below.

Outside the scant protection of the tent the night closed in. The thin air wracked his lungs and drained his spirit. The mean wind whined against the frozen rocks. Somewhere across on the ridge was where so much mountaineering history had been made; where Colonel Norton had clambered to within a gasp of the summit and then retreated, and where Odell, a dot down there, had peered through his telescope to glimpse Mallory and Irvine climbing to their deaths. For a mountaineer these could have been momentous thoughts but they did not occur to Messner, as he curled up like a hibernating animal, overcome by infinite tiredness and the numbing cold.

Slowly the light filtered into the tent, through the rattling canvas and frozen spindrift. He felt even worse, but to remain in this place offered only deterioration and death. He dragged himself from the tent and, leaving everything except his climbing equipment and camera, began a steep diagonal descent of the North Face.

*   *   *

The sound of a stream rushing from the glacier and of a raven croaking and flapping its wings on a rock near the camp were all that kept Nena company as she studied the lower slopes of the mountain through the telescopic lens of her camera. There was nothing, no sign of life on that blinding wilderness. It was a beautiful morning, warm and sunny. She washed in the freezing water of the stream.

Time was ticking by and anxiety was beginning to snipe at her. It had been easy to talk with Reinhold about what to do if he did not reappear. That had been in the abstract because he had been standing there in front of her. She could reach out and touch him. Now the mountain was empty; she had no idea where he was or how far he had reached. She turned to walk away from the stream. In the corner of her eye a dark dot moved at the top of the North Col. She blinked; it was still there. A kind of wild excitement sent her into a panic. She burst into tears.

Even at that distance she could see that Messner was not moving with his usual, loose-limbed stride. He moved down from the North Col like a drunk man, a stumbling replica of the climber who had set out four mornings earlier. He came across the glacier very slowly, moving like a robot or a mechanical doll, looking up only once. He glanced quickly at Nena. His head was slumped forward and his movements were hardly conscious.

"Reinhold, wie geht's?" Nena said and heard the quiet sobs in reply.

"It's okay, Reinhold, you are going to be fine. The camp is right here," she said holding him and feeling that she had never been so close to anyone.

"But where are all my friends?" Reinhold asked, half delirious.

"I'm your friend. I'm here. Don't worry."

He looked at her, his eyes brimming with tears. His face was yellow, his lips swollen, cracked and smeared with pus. Heat stroke was surely affecting him.

Nena took his rucksack, handed him another ski stick with which to support himself and led the way off the glacier to the camp. The reality of being secure drained the nervous tension from his wracked sun-scorched body. His mind accepted that he was safe. He had achieved his highest, his most impossible ambition.

Epilogue

THE LION AND THE LAMB

AFTER TWICE CLIMBING Everest, each time in daring style, it is reasonable to ask "what next?" Surely life must seem empty for a professional mountaineer who has achieved such a summit, in every sense, especially for a man whose fame might be thought to rely upon building continually from one remarkable achievement to another yet more remarkable.

But there never will be a "last great problem" in mountain climbing, for, as one last face, peak, traverse or challenge is overcome so another emerges across an infinite horizon. And to Reinhold Messner mountains have become an almost incidental part of his lifestyle. He has developed a natural skill at climbing rock and ice and adapting to the rigours of high altitude. That is his gift, and with words and pictures he can communicate adventure to a ready market; though as a personal experience he would claim that the so-called "conquering" of a mountain hardly registers.

Climbing has become for him an act of introspection, of watching, almost dispassionately, how he himself reacts to the extreme circumstances into which mountaineering puts him. Just as adversity may heighten the relationship between people, many years of calculated risk and sensing the brittle reality of danger have brought to Messner a deep affinity with mountains. He does not conquer them or collect them, although to the artless eye that may seem to be the case; he simply enjoys their company, is highly proficient at climbing them and has been extraordinarily lucky.

That is why Everest in no sense leaves a vacuum in Messner's life. He has a powerful wish to achieve, and that lies behind his adventures.

Few things are more ephemeral than footprints on the summit of an 8,000 metre peak, and only the climber can really know the exhaustion and fear he had to overcome to get there, or the skill and good luck it took for him to return safely. Just as some people find it impossible to accept that life exists without some mystical force underpinning it, so Messner rejects that climbing mountains is no more than a simple act of going to

167

the top and back. The exhilaration of achieving something new and the self-awareness that comes from pushing out to the furthest physical limits have, as a reward, a curious serenity. As a simple ambition, he would probably like to become the first man to climb all the 8,000 metre peaks in the world, and indeed he is further towards achieving that goal than any other climber.

Nena Holguin has lived with Reinhold for more than a year and has come to know the cold wrath and the warm affection of this mercurial man as well as anyone. The child whose "retribution was extreme" has carried the characteristic into manhood and that has won him an unfair reputation for being obdurate and abrupt. His close friends reject that view of him, although many have seen his wild, stentorian rages that occasionally explode. In the close quarters of a mountaineering expedition when exhaustion, thin air, fear and ambition all help to sharpen any antagonism that develops, the strain in relationships quickly becomes exaggerated.

Reinhold's determination, Nena Holguin says, is legendary not only when it is applied to climbing mountains. If he is convinced he is right about an issue, nothing will change his mind. On an early trek that he led to Mount Noshaq in the Himalayas a group of wild-tempered Balti porters went on strike half a day's walk from base camp. They threw down their loads, declared they were already at base camp and demanded payment. Messner went ahead alone, found the proper camp site and hurried back. He patiently explained the camp was a little further on but the hundred or so Balti porters stubbornly refused to budge.

Rage boiling inside him, Messner ordered the porters to pile the loads into a large pyramid. Grasping an ice axe in one hand and a large stick in the other he climbed to the top of the pile and bellowed at the porters, telling them that unless they shifted the loads they would not be paid. Murderous looks were exchanged. Messner threatened to slaughter the first man who laid a hand on the loads. The porters were clearly impressed at the strength behind the threat for they grumblingly picked up their packs and tramped on. Since then he has again had reason to be angry with porters, spectacularly so on the South Col of Everest when arguably he saved their lives by terrifying them into action. But largely he enjoys their company, shares their humour and respects their society.

Messner's strongest wrath is directed at anyone who tried to take advantage of him. The commercial side of his nature that worked to turn his expeditions into profit was balanced by a generosity in organising small-scale expeditions to Nepal or Pakistan and inviting young talented climbers to go at no expense to themselves.

"He puts the whole of himself into these trips and usually they work out well, but occasionally someone perhaps accuses Reinhold of not allowing them enough public mention, or openly criticises him unjustly. If they do, they are digging themselves a grave," Nena says.

That sore of futile disagreement was irrelevant to the small isolated world of the solitary mountaineer bivouacked high on the flank of an 8,000 metre peak, sipping a salty brew of Tibetan tea with the entire world beneath his feet. Messner always found that "someone" kept him company at such altitudes: an awareness of another person, a partner within himself. Nena wrote: "Sometimes I feel so squelched by this man, but then I know that is what I want anyway — a strong man, a single separate identity.

"I know that sometimes speed is essential for safety in mountains; it may even mean the difference between survival and a close risk of death. I'm aware of this in safe mountaineering but what I'm saying about Reinhold is quite different. It is some compelling force, something inside him that you cannot separate from him. It makes him the way he is. Perhaps it is what enables him to climb over 8,000 metres alone and without question. It is present in all his actions, everything he does. It is not just in the mountains but everywhere: Lhasa, Peking, all the way back to Europe on the lecture tours. It is a relentless, driving energy." The lion and the lamb, close together.

CHRONOLOGY
LIST OF BOOKS
INDEX

CHRONOLOGY

1944   Born, 17th September. Childhood and early school days at St. Peter, Villnöss.

1949   Climbed south face of Saas Rigais, Geisler Alps.

1951–63   Hundreds of climbs in local mountains and Dolomites.

1958   Went to High School in Bolzano.

1965   First ascent of Ortler north wall.

1966   Walker Spur, Grandes Jorasses.

1967   First Grade 6 solo, the Solda on Piz Ciavazes.
Mount Agner north face, first winter ascent.
Furchetta north wall, first winter ascent.
Taught maths at Eppan school.
Padua University.

1968   First ascent Heiligkreuzkofel, Mittel-Pfeiler.
Eiger north pillar, first ascent.
Marmolata south wall direct, first ascent.

1969   Austrian expedition to the Andes.
Les Droites north wall, first solo ascent.
Philipp-Flamm route on Civetta, first solo ascent.
Marmolata di Rocca, south wall direct, first solo ascent.
Langkofel, north wall direct, first ascent.
Studies at Padua complete.

1970   Nanga Parbat expedition. Günther is killed on descent of Diamir face.
Recovery from frost bite and return to teaching maths at Eppan school.

1971	Expeditions to Persia, Nepal, New Guinea, Pakistan (Nanga Parbat) and East Africa. New routes in Dolomites and in the Carstenz mountains.
1972	Manaslu south wall, first ascent. Noshaq in Hindu Kush.
1973	Several first ascents in Dolomites. Pelmo north-west wall. Marmolata west pillar. Furchetta west wall. Journey to Nanga Parbat.
1974	Aconcagua south wall, first ascent. Makalu expedition fails. Eiger north wall in ten hours. Matterhorn north wall.
1975	Lhotse south face attempt. Success with Peter Habeler on Hidden Peak in Karakoram.
1976	Mt. McKinley, first ascent of Midnight Sun wall. Ortler west pillar, first ascent. Annapurna expedition fails. Climbs in Japan.
1977	Dhaulagiri south wall attempt. Uschi and Reinhold separate.
1978	East African expedition and first ascent of Breach Wall, Kilimanjaro. Everest without oxygen. Nanga Parbat solo.
1979	Rescue on Ama Dablam. K2, the second highest summit.
1980	Everest, solo.

BOOKS BY REINHOLD MESSNER

Bergvölker der Erde, Athesia, Bozen.

Grenzbereich Todeszone, Kiepenheuer und Witsch, Cologne.

Die Extremen, fünf jahrzehnte sechster Grad, B L V Verlagsgesellschaft, Munich.

Aufbruch ins Abenteuer, Athesia, Bozen.

Klettersteige Dolomiten, Athesia, Bozen.

Klettersteige Ostalpen, Athesia, Bozen.

Der 7 Grad extremstes Bergsteigen, B L V, Munich, 1973; *The Seventh Grade: Most Extreme Climbing*, Kaye & Ward Ltd, 1974.

Der Herausforderung, B L V, Munich, 1976; *The Challenge*, Kaye & Ward Ltd, 1977.

Die grossen Wände, B L V, Munich, 1977; *The Big Walls*, Kaye & Ward Ltd, 1978.

Arena der Einsamkeit, Athesia, Bozen.

Zurück in die Berge, Bildband von Ernst Pertl, Athesia, Bozen.

Die rote Rakete am Nange Parbat.

Sturm am Manaslu, B L V, Munich.

Everest – Expedition zum Endpunkt, B L V, Munich, 1978; *Everest: Expedition to the Ultimate*, Kaye & Ward Ltd, 1979.

Alleingang Nange Parbat, B L V, Munich, 1979; *Solo Nanga Parbat*, Kaye & Ward Ltd, 1980.

K2: Berg der Berge, B L V, Munich, 1980; *K2: Mountain of Mountains* Kaye & Ward Ltd, 1981.

INDEX

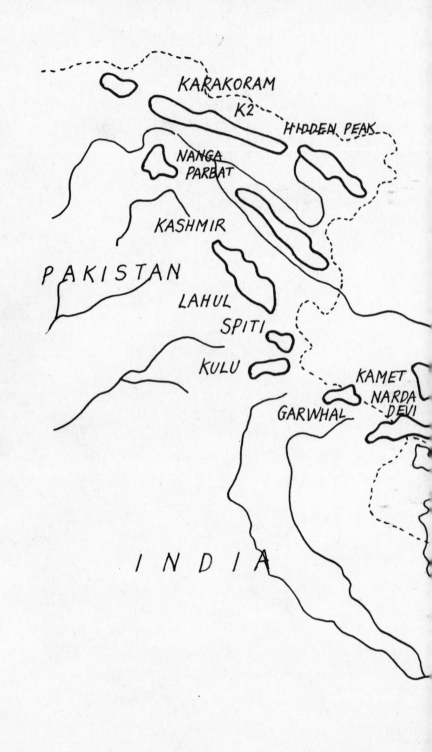